To my parents
Clarence and Marjorie Shepherd

Contents

Foreword

Acknowledgments

Part I
A Short History of Sailors' Snug Harbor

14 Embarkation (1801-1833)

18 The Early Years
Rum Drinkers and Religion (1834-1864)

22 Expansion and Controversy (1865-1898)

28 Halcyon Years (1899-1940)

32 Modernization and Retrenchment (1941-1976)

Part II
38 **Snug Harbor Album**

Part III
Snug Harbor Anthology

71 Introduction

72 "The Sailors' Snug Harbor," *Harper's New Monthly Magazine*, January 1873.

76 "When the Sails Are Furled" by Theodore Dreiser, from *The Color of a Great City*, 1927.

82 "Old Cap Knowles" and "Gaff Topsail Ben Breeze" by Frank Waters, from *Eight Bells: Sailors' Snug Harbor Yarns and Ballads*, 1927.

94 Selections from *When Ships Were Ships and Not Tin Pots* by William Morris Barnes, 1930.

104 Bibliography

Barnett Shepherd

Sailors' Snug Harbor
1801-1976

SECOND EDITION

Snug Harbor Cultural Center
Staten Island, New York

Copyright © 1979 Barnett Shepherd
All rights reserved

Library of Congress Cataloging in Publication Data

Shepherd, Barnett, 1938-
    Sailors' Snug Harbor, 1801-1976.

    Bibliography: p.
    1. New York (State). Sailors' Snug Harbor—
History. I. Title.
HV3035.N6S5   362.8'5   79-16979

Designed by Anthony McCall

Produced by the Publishing Center for
Cultural Resources, New York City

Second printing (1995) produced by
Furthermore Press, Germantown, New York

Selections from *The Color of a Great City* are reprinted by permission of the Dreiser Trust. Selections from *Eight Bells* are reprinted by permission of Hawthorne Press.

Illustrations

1. Map of Manhattan Island, 1777
"Plan of the City of New York in North America Surveyed in Years 1776 and 1777 by Bernard Ratzer, Lieutenant in 60th Regiment of Foot." New-York Historical Society, New York City.

2. Manhattan Island and the Harbor, 1794
Engraving by Saint-Memin, "View of the City and Harbor of New York, Taken From Mount Pitt, the Seat of John R. Livingston, Esqre." New-York Historical Society, New York City.

3. Last Will and Testament of Robert Richard Randall, 1801
Manuscript courtesy of Trustees Sailors' Snug Harbor.

4. Map of the Trustees' Property, 1801
Manuscript map "A Figurative Plan of the Estate belonging to Cap. Randall in the Seventh Ward of the City of New York October 26, 1801 Surveyed by Joseph Fr. Mangin City Surveyor, No. 301 Greenwich Street." Snug Harbor Cultural Center.

5. Trustees' Seal
Design by Robertson, 1806.

6. Map of New York City, 1827
"A New Map of the City of New York Comprising All the Late Improvements, Compiled and Corrected from Authentic Documents. Designed to Accompany the Description of New York." New-York Historical Society, New York City.

7. Map of the Trustees' Property, 1830
Manuscript map "New York May 1830 surveyed by Thomas R. Ludlam, City Surveyor." Snug Harbor Cultural Center.

8. 15 Washington Square North
Scrapbook photograph. Local History and Genealogy Division, New York Public Library, Main Branch.

9. A. T. Stewart's Store, 1869
Engraving in *Shannon's Manual of Common Council.* New-York Historical Society, New York City.

10. Washington Square, c.1940
Photograph, Local History and Genealogy Division, New York Public Library, Main Branch.

11. New York Bay, 1856
"Map of the Bay & Harbor of New York." Staten Island Institute of Arts and Sciences.

12. Sailors' Snug Harbor, 1833
Woodcut by Elisha Forbes in *Sailors' Magazine and Naval Journal,* (September 1, 1833). New-York Historical Society, New York City.

13. New Brighton, 1838
Engraving by Rolph, after a painting by Chapman, in *Richmond County Mirror,* Vol. I, 1838. Staten Island Institute of Arts and Sciences.

14. Sailors' Snug Harbor, 1842
Frontispiece, copper engraving by James Narine and Co., from, *Copy of the Last Will and Testament of Robert Richard Randall.* Butler Library, Columbia University.

15. Sailors' Snug Harbor, 1898
Watercolor by H. M. Pettit in *Leslie's Weekly* (August 12, 1899). Boston Public Library.

16. Sailors' Snug Harbor, 1907
Plate 2 from *Atlas of the Borough of Richmond, City of New York,* E. Robinson. Staten Island Institute of Arts and Sciences.

17. Waterfront, c.1884
Photograph of Steamboat *Thomas W. Hunt* unloading at Snug Harbor. Staten Island Historical Society.

18. Dock House, c.1910
Postcard. Staten Island Institute of Arts and Sciences.

19. Gatehouse, c.1910
Postcard. Staten Island Institute of Arts and Sciences.

20. Sailors' Snug Harbor, 1884
Lithograph by C. H. Reed in *Century Magazine* (June, 1884). Staten Island Institute of Arts and Sciences.

21. Sailors' Snug Harbor, c.1920
Unidentified photographic clipping. Davis Collection, Staten Island Institute of Arts and Sciences.

22. Sailors' Snug Harbor, c.1900
Photograph by Edward Clegg. Staten Island Historical Society.

23. Admission of an Old Sailor to the Harbor, 1873
Woodcut by Phineas F. Annin in *Harper's New Monthly Magazine* (January, 1873). Staten Island Institute of Arts and Sciences.

24. One of the Sleeping-Rooms, 1873
Woodcut by Phineas F. Annin in *Harper's New Monthly Magazine* (January, 1873). Staten Island Institute of Arts and Sciences.

25. Bedroom, 1916
Photograph by Edwin Levick in *New York Tribune* (November 26, 1916). Staten Island Institute of Arts and Sciences.

26. Hallway Outside Dining Room, c.1910
Postcard. Staten Island Institute of Arts and Sciences.

27. The Dining Room, 1916
Photograph by Edwin Levick in *New York Tribune* (November 26, 1916). Staten Island Institute of Arts and Sciences.

28. Workroom, 1873
Woodcut by Phineas F. Annin in *Harper's New Monthly Magazine* (January, 1873). Staten Island Institute of Arts and Sciences.

29. Workroom, 1884
Lithograph in *Century Magazine* (June, 1884). Staten Island Institute of Arts and Sciences.

30. Workroom, 1882
Engraving by T. de Thulstrup, in *Harper's Weekly* (August 12, 1882). Staten Island Historical Society.

31. Workroom, c.1900
Photograph by Edward Clegg in Trustees' Sailors' Snug Harbor Photograph Album.

32. The Reading Room, 1937
Photograph by Edward Otto Lindeman in *New York Herald Tribune* (September 5, 1937). Staten Island Institute of Arts and Sciences.

33. The Library, 1937
Photograph by Edward Otto Lindeman in *New York Herald Tribune* (September 5, 1937). Staten Island Institute of Arts and Sciences.

34. The Chapel, 1876
Lithograph, frontispiece, Copy of the Last Will and Testament of Robert Richard Randall. Staten Island Institute of Arts and Sciences.

35. Chapel Interior, 1975
Photograph by Eric Aerts. Staten Island Institute of Arts and Sciences.

36. The Chapel, 1886
Lithograph by C. Hyatt in *Illustrated Sketch Book of Staten Island, New York.* Staten Island Institute of Arts and Sciences.

37. The Randall Memorial Church, 1899
Photograph in *American Architect and Building News* (October 25, 1899). Avery Fine Arts Library, Columbia University.

38. Church Interior, 1899
Photograph in *American Architect and Building News* (October 25, 1899). Avery Fine Arts Library, Columbia University.

39. The Randall Memorial Church and Music Hall, c.1900
Photograph by Edward Clegg in Trustees' Sailors' Snug Harbor Photograph Album.

40. Music Hall Interior, c.1930
Photograph. Staten Island Institute of Arts and Sciences. Gift of Trustees' Sailors' Snug Harbor.

41. Sanitorium Interior, c.1901
Photograph by Edward Clegg in Trustees' Sailors' Snug Harbor Photograph Album.

42. Sailors' Snug Harbor, with Hospital in Foreground, c.1930
Photograph. Snug Harbor Cultural Center.

43. Sanitorium, 1904
Photograph in *The Sunday Magazine, New York Tribune* (May 22, 1904). Staten Island Historical Society.

44. The Governor's House, c.1910
Postcard. Staten Island Institute of Arts and Sciences.

45. Road Leading to the Graveyard, 1979
Photograph by Bill Kushmick.

46. Graveyard, 1979
Photograph by Bill Kushmick.

47. Air View, 1931
Photograph by Fairchild Aerial Survey, October, 1931. Snug Harbor Cultural Center.

48. Randall Memorial Church Demolition, 1952
Photograph by Barry Schwartz in *Staten Island Advance* (September 11, 1952). Staten Island Institute of Arts and Sciences.

49. Front Buildings, Rear Elevation, c.1966
Photograph, Snug Harbor Cultural Center.

50. Front Buildings, 1973
Photograph by Barnett Shepherd.

51. Fence, 1973
Photograph by Barnett Shepherd.

52. Dome, Main Hall, 1975
Photograph by Eric Aerts. Staten Island Institute of Arts and Sciences.

53. Recreation Hall Interior, 1975
Photograph by Eric Aerts. Staten Island Institute of Arts and Sciences.

Page 30: Main Hall, 1975
Photograph by Eric Aerts. Staten Island Institute of Arts and Sciences.

Section Titles

Part I **Field with Chapel and Music Hall in the Distance, 1979**
Photograph by Bill Kushmick.

Part II **Sailors' Snug Harbor, 1853**
Woodcut by J. W. Orr in *The National Magazine* (October 1853). Staten Island Institute of Arts and Sciences.

Part III **Bedroom, 1916**
Photograph by Edwin Levick in *New York Tribune* (November 26, 1916). Staten Island Institute of Arts and Sciences.

Cover: Workroom, 1882
Detail. Engraving by T. de Thulstrup, in *Harper's Weekly* (August 12, 1882). Staten Island Historical Society.

Foreword

I first encountered Snug Harbor one cold February evening. Walking through the west gatehouse with the Greek Revival Buildings in the distance amid freshly fallen snow. I felt I was going back in time. There was something very peaceful and orderly about Snug Harbor. In the main hall, that great Eastlake interior reminiscent of a ship's saloon, I could envision people listening to a chamber recital or viewing an historic exhibit. The unequaled potential of Snug Harbor as a visual and performing arts facility mixed in my mind with images of the generations of seamen who once lived there.

Barnett Shepherd's study of the first 175 years of Sailor's Snug Harbor represents a comprehensive look at the men who built, administered, and inhabited one of America's oldest health and welfare institutions. His research adds to our awareness of the central role played by the sea in our cultural and economic development. The Greek Revival, Italianate, and Beaux Arts structures at Snug Harbor mark the grown of American maritime power.

Sailors' Snug Harbor: 1801-1976 is being published jointly by the Snug Harbor Cultural Center and the Staten Island Institute of Arts and Sciences. The Institute provided leadership in the early years to help achieve landmark status for the buildings and encouraged the development of the site as a cultural center. It will relocate at the Harbor in 1982. The Cultural Center is privileged to assist in publishing a history of this important American landmark site.

Some extraordinary people, under the leadership of Elizabeth Robinson, have come forward to make this publication possible. They are the real publishers of this volume: Jane S. Aberlin, Terence and Gloria Benbow, Mr. & Mrs. Richard Diamond, Mr. & Mrs. Bruce Evans, Mrs. Robert M. Leng, Rev. George D. McClain, Rev. Tilda Norberg, Mr. & Mrs. J. Bay Robinson, Dr. & Mrs. Albert Roland, Mr. & Mrs. Clarence H. Shepherd, Jr., Dorothy Valentine Smith, Meredith Sykes, and Shirley Zavin.

All of us at Snug Harbor and especially those concerned about our national architectural heritage salute these friends of Snug Harbor.

Michael Terrence Sheehan
Executive Director
Snug Harbor Cultural Center
March 1979

Foreword to Second Edition

The saga of the Snug Harbor Cultural Center is the second chapter in the life of this remarkable site and this legend is added to every day. The first chapter is the story of what we have inherited and can be found in this book which Barnett Shephard has so thoroughly documented. The reasons for the creation of what we know as Snug Harbor as well as what happened on this site during the 175 years when it was the home for retired sailors can be found here, told in a remarkably lively and interesting fashion. We are lucky to have this history recorded for us and for future generations, and we are happy to be involved in the production of the second edition.

A great deal has happened at Snug Harbor Cultural Center since this book was first published in 1979. An aggressive campaign was undertaken to stabilize and preserve the buildings making the site more hospitable to additional arts organizations. The Staten Island Children's Museum, the Staten Island Botanical Garden, the John Noble Collection, and the Art Lab joined a host of smaller arts organizations in calling the site home. In addition, nearly forty individual artists are now occupying studio space and are working and creating an excitement felt throughout the campus. Much of the original potential seen by the founding members of the Center has been met, but there is now as even greater potential for the use of this unique site. It has been proven that a complex of this size can be adapted for reuse as a center devoted to culture, but the depth of possible offerings has barely been tested. As we approach our twentieth year as a cultural institution of the city of New York, there is much more work to do, but the surroundings, the people, this history, and the art itself make the task a pleasure.

David E. Kleiser
President & CEO
Snug Harbor Cultural Center
January 1995

Acknowledgments

I would like to thank the following people for their assistance:

Above all, Dr. Shirley Zavin for her editorial assistance in giving form to this text and for her encouragement throughout the project.

The good people at Shalom House, Clinton Avenue, Staten Island, where I resided during 1973-1975 while researching and writing this book—George McClain, Tilda Norberg, Miriam Crist, Cindy Read, Margo Koch Ruthe, Faith Hagenhofer, Harlan Bemis and Bruce Bramlett.

The staff of the Staten Island Institute of Arts and Sciences, particularly George O. Pratt, Jr., former Director of the Staten Island Museum, whose interest in Snug Harbor encouraged me to begin this study; Henry Korn, who assisted me with a grant application; Librarian Gail Schneider, who brought forward many historic materials; Research Associate Hugh Powell, who shared his knowledge of Staten Island history; and Dennis Schneider, for his photographic work.

Captain Leo Kraszeski, Administrator, Sailors' Snug Harbor, for permission to read the Harbor's Minute Books and other archival materials; Captain James Ross, who gave access to the buildings at Snug Harbor; Comptroller George McCracken for providing access to the Harbor records in his 262 Greene Street office over a period of many months; and his colleagues Donald Brink and Carolyn Schwartz.

Carlin Gasteyer, former Planning Director, Snug Harbor Cultural Center, who generously made available her copy of Don G. Seitz's manuscript on Snug Harbor, which was an invaluable resource.

The staff of the Local History Division, New York Public Library, Fifth Avenue Branch; Staff of the Library and Print Room, New-York Historical Society, New York City; Loring McMillen and Harlow McMillen of the Staten Island Historical Society; Douglas Whiddon, former Librarian, Seamen's Church Institute; Adolf K. Placzek, Librarian, Avery Fine Arts Library, Columbia University; Carlyle R. Bennett, former Director, Municipal Archives; Jerome A. Mardison, Reference Librarian, College of Staten Island; Les Trautmann, Managing Editor, *Staten Island Advance;* and Mrs. Herbert Magruder, Snug Harbor neighbor, who shared her memories of the institution.

Michael Terrence Sheehan, Executive Director, Snug Harbor Cultural Center and A. Mae Seeley, Administrator of the Staten Island Institute of Arts and Sciences, for their assistance in arranging publication of this volume.

Barnett Shepherd
Staten Island, 1979

Field with Chapel and Music Hall in the Distance, 1979

Part I
A Short History of
Sailors' Snug Harbor

Embarkation (1801-1833)

Opening on August 1, 1833, Sailors' Snug Harbor on Staten Island, New York, is America's first and most famous home for retired seamen.* The story of its founding begins much earlier, however, with the history of a family whose fortune was made from the sea.

Thomas Randall, the family's patriarch, immigrated to New York from Scotland in the 1740s. He quickly established himself as a ship owner, merchant and privateer, a career which amassed him a substantial fortune. During the Seven Years War (1756-1763), which in this country pitted the French against the English and was known as the French and Indian War, Randall was given permission by the English Crown to capture French ships. America, still a colonial nation, controlled no warships, but armed private vessels like those owned by Randall played an important part in the English war effort by preying on the French as they traded with Quebec and their West Indian possessions. Randall at one time owned at least three such vessels; one called *The Fox* was a sloop with fourteen guns and one hundred men.

Profits from this "honest" privateering founded Randall's fortune, and his knowledge of the sea and business skills multiplied it throughout his life.

He became an important figure in New York City's civic life. With his son Thomas, Jr., Randall joined with a group of colonial merchants in 1770 in organizing the Marine Society of the City of New York under a Charter granted by George III. Randall drew up the articles of association and served as second vice president. The goal of the Society's members, recruited from the ranks of the city's most influential citizens, was to "improve maritime knowledge" and to relieve indigent and distressed shipmasters, their orphans and widows.

Thomas Randall later served on New York's Committees of Fifty-One and One Hundred, which were instrumental in convening the New York Colonial Congress, one of the events that led toward American Independence. Randall and his family fled from occupied

---

*The U.S. Naval Asylum at Philadelphia, the first of several hospitals founded by the Navy, but the only one specifically for *retired* sailors, opened in 1834, one year after Snug Harbor. Sailors' Snug Harbor in Boston, a private benefaction closely paralleling Randall's endowment, opened its doors in 1854. Following an Act of Congress in 1865 a number of naval and military asylums for retired veterans opened throughout the United States.

There appears to be no documented history of institutions founded specifically for the aged. With its conception in Randall's will of 1801, Snug Harbor may rank as the oldest institution in America founded for that purpose.

New York City as did many patriot merchants, and settled on a farm near Chatham, New Jersey. After the city was vacated by the British, he returned from exile. His name heads a list of citizens greeting General Washington upon his entrance to the city on November 25, 1783. Randall served on the first Board of Aldermen of the liberated city and was a founding member of the Chamber of Commerce. On the day of Washington's inauguration in 1789 Randall served as the coxswain of the ceremonial boat he had designed to convey the newly elected President from Elizabethport, New Jersey, to the ceremonies in New York City.

Randall received from the sea not only his fortune and respected civic status, but personal tragedy as well. His oldest son, a mercantile trader like his father, died at sea in 1772. The following report from the *New York Gazette and Weekly Mercury* tells of the loss:

> Last Wednesday Capt. Thomas Randle Jun., of this port, inward bound from the West Indies, a few miles from Sandy Hook, was knocked overboard with the Boom and drowned. He was a promising youth, and his death is greatly lamented by all his acquaintances.

Years later in 1797 when Randall died at his residence at 7 Whitehall Street, his will provided that his estate be divided equally between the three surviving children, Catherine, Paul and Robert. Catherine married after her father's death and lived in Chatham, New Jersey. Paul died a pauper in France.

Although it is Robert Randall who is most important to the history of Snug Harbor, so little is known of his life that we must imagine he lived modestly in the shadow of his father. He joined the Marine Society in 1771, one year after his father and older brother, and for a time was in business with his father and Alexander Stewart under the name "Randall & Son and Stewart." He was a member of the Tontine Coffee House, a merchants' rendezvous of that day, and later a subscriber to the New York Society Library. At the outbreak of the Revolution he petitioned the Provincial Congress to join the First Battalion, admitting, however, that he was "totally unacquainted" with military affairs. In 1790 he took up residence at a twenty-one-acre farm his father had just purchased on Manhattan Island, two miles north of the city limits. (Fig. 1.) There, surrounded by servants and enjoying the life of a bachelor gentleman farmer, Robert survived his father by four years.*

By far his most famous deed—and the one by which he is remembered today—occurred on June 1, 1801, when he signed his will. Without any immediate heirs he sought a meaningful use of the wealth he and his father had gained from the sea. He directed that his assets be used to "erect...upon some eligible part of the land upon which I now reside, an Asylum, or Marine Hospital, to be called 'Sailors' Snug Harbor' for the purpose of maintaining and supporting aged, decrepit and worn-out sailors." He also provided annuities for any children that his surviving brother Paul might have. To Betsey Hart, his housekeeper, he gave an annuity and his gold sleeve buttons; to Adam Shields, his overseer, his gold watch and forty pounds; and to another servant his shoe and knee buckles. All the remaining assets and land would be used for the Harbor.

We do not know precisely why Randall decided to endow a "Snug Harbor," for there are no clues provided in the will. A later tradition ascribed the idea to Alexander Hamilton, an acquaintance of the Randall family. The legend states that Randall summoned Hamilton at the time he made his will to ask what should be done with the estate. Hamilton suggested that since it had been earned from the sea, it should be returned to the sea. Although we know Randall's sister Catherine had sought Hamilton's advice concerning her father's estate five years earlier, there is no recorded evidence to indicate he gave assistance to Robert. Regardless of the source of inspiration—a suggestion by Hamilton or Robert himself—the will did succeed in returning to the sea what had come from the sea.

At the time Randall wrote his will there was a definite need for an institution that could provide care for retired and disabled sailors. Although a fund had been started by Congress in 1794 to build a naval asylum for merchant and naval seamen, the U.S. Navy, which was only three years old in 1801, had not yet established a marine hospital. The only precedent for an institution dedicated to the care of aged seamen was the Royal Hospital at Greenwich, England. By Randall's day it was a venerable and famous institution. Founded in 1694 by William and Mary as a "thank offering" for naval victories, by 1801 it provided care for nearly two thousand naval pensioners in its palatial buildings along the banks of the Thames. It is quite possible that the Royal Hospital was known to Randall and that he intended his farm and

---

*Much information about Randall and his family was found in *The Sailors' Snug Harbor: a History of Captain Robert Richard Randall's Foundation for the Toilers of the Sea* by Donald C. Seitz (1958), an unpublished manuscript in possession of the Board of Trustees of Sailors' Snug Harbor.

property be used to create an American "Greenwich." It would be an appropriate thank offering for the wealth his father had gained from the sea and the toil of sailors. Although he does not say so in his will, we may further speculate that it may also have been intended as a memorial to his father and his older brother.

Randall knew of the Marine Society's benevolent work for shipmasters, since he was a member of that group, but his own endowment was more broadly conceived than either the Society or the Greenwich Hospital. Sailors of any rank or nationality, naval or merchant seamen, were all equally eligible to become residents of the new community.

Randall's will names eight Trustees of the Snug Harbor, who were also to serve as executors of his will. They were the following New York office holders and their successors: The Chancellor of the State of New York, the Mayor of the City of New York, the Recorder of the City, the President of the Chamber of Commerce, the President and Vice President of the Marine Society, the Senior Minister of the Episcopal Church (later to be established as the Rector of Trinity Church) and the Senior Minister of the Presbyterian Church (later to be established as the Minister of the First Presbyterian Church). Randall died June 5, 1801, four days after signing his will, leaving his estate in very good hands.

No activity resulted from Randall's action until 1806, when the Trustees met to incorporate. They established by-laws for the corporation and commissioned a seal of the institution. (Fig. 3.) In the next two decades, a number of claims to Randall's fortune had to be adjudicated. By the time the last suit was settled by the U.S. Supeme Court in 1830—a suit brought by an Episcopal Bishop of Nova Scotia claiming to be Randall's descendant on his mother's side—Randall's farm bounded what by then had become the northern edge of a rapidly expanding city. (Fig. 4.) The Trustees had received permission from the state legislature in 1828 to locate the institution further from the city, while holding the original farm—today a site bordering Manhattan's Washington Square—to produce income for the trust. The farmland was graded, streets laid through it and building lots marked for leasing. (Fig. 5.) The Trustees began to look for a quieter location for the Snug Harbor and in May 1831 purchased the 130-acre Isaac Housman farm on the north shore of Staten Island. The fertile land, an abundant supply of spring water and a view of New York harbor and the shipping along the Kill van Kull made the farm an ideal site. The neighborhood adjoining the farm was soon to be developed as a fashionable summer resort called New Brighton.

The Trustees quickly made plans to erect a building upon their land. In May 1831 they placed an advertisement in the *New York Mercantile Advertiser* stating that "a premium of Fifty Dollars would be paid for a plan of an asylum to be constructed of brick or stone and to afford accommodations for two hundred men." In July work was begun on a dock for the property. Meeting at the Mayor's office on July 30, the Trustees reviewed the plans submitted in response to their advertisement, selected the one drawn by Minard Lafever, a carpenter and draftsman, and awarded him the fifty-dollar premium.

Lafever was just beginning his architectural career. He would later design several important Brooklyn churches and gain much fame as the author of planbooks and texts on architecture. The Snug Harbor building is Lafever's earliest known work, and like many important buildings of the time it is in the Greek Revival style. As his model for the portico of the building Lafever selected a drawing from Stuart and Revett's *Antiquities of Athens* (1796) of a Greek temple on the Ilyssus River near Athens. Following the fashion of the day Captain Randall's beneficiaries were to be housed in the style of ancient Greece, an indication that it was a proud institution with important plans for the future.

In late August or September delivery of building materials began. A shipment of 19,800 feet of "yellow pine flooring boards," arrived on September 23 and on the following day came 46,000 bricks, the first of more than 500,000 needed for the building. Stone for the building was quarried by state prisoners at Sing Sing in Ossining, New York, and shipped on barges down the Hudson to the new Snug Harbor dock.

As the building neared completion in the summer of 1833 the Trustees placed an advertisement in the *New York Gazette & General Advertiser* in preparation for opening the institution:

> Sailors' Snug Harbor—the building on Staten Island will be in readiness to receive a limited number of aged, decrepit & worn out SAILORS, on the 1st day of August next. Applications for admittance to be made on & after the 4th of July, to the committee, at No. 12 James' Bldgs. No. 48 Wall St. from 12 to 2 o'clock, on Tuesdays & Fridays.

Thirty-seven men had been enrolled when the Harbor opened with formal religious ceremonies on August 1, 1833. (Fig. 9.) The number of residents increased steadily each year thereafter.

In 1834 Robert Randall's bones were removed from

the graveyard of Saint-Mark's-in-the-Bowery, placed "in a new case," as the Trustees' *Minutes* report, and taken by private carriage and steamboat to the Snug Harbor dock. The residents, "cleanly dressed in blue jackets and white trousers," waited at the dock, followed the casket in silent procession and placed it beneath the monument in front of the main building. Willow trees were later planted on either side of the monument and the memorial to Randall was complete.

Robert Randall's vision of a "Snug Harbor" for "aged, decrepit and worn-out sailors" had finally become a reality thirty-three years after his death.

The Early Years
Rum Drinkers and Religion
(1834-1864)

Since Randall left no directives to guide the institution, it was the Trustees who were responsible for its development and growth. Without existing models, daily life at Snug Harbor was shaped not only by the nature and needs of its earliest residents, but also by the attitudes and values of its administrators. Reconciling the often divergent interests of these two groups proved to be a continuing challenge for the developing institution.

Randall's words "aged, decrepit and worn-out" reflect the fact that a sailor's life was extremely difficult. Its hardships were gradually brought to public attention in the nineteenth century, partially through the publication of Richard Henry Dana's *Two Years Before the Mast* and other narratives of the sea. The physical hazards of life at sea—constant exposure to harsh weather, long hours, inadequate living quarters, dangerous working conditions and poorly balanced diets—all too often produced sailors "worn-out" before their time. The recorded ailments of the first sailors admitted to Snug Harbor are vivid testimony to that. Seven of the original thirty-seven had lost a leg, two were blind, another lame, another frost-bitten, four described as decrepit and five as rheumatic.

In addition, the behavior patterns learned at sea did not always translate easily to a different setting. The rigid and authoritarian structure of shipboard society and the traditional codes of conduct that regulated all activities did not encourage the development of independence and self-sufficiency. The traditional "sailors' sprees"—the excessive drinking and carousing on shore fueled by weeks of confinement in cramped quarters and made possible by the receipt of their wages—were at odds with the mores of a land-bound society. Thrift was an uncommon virtue for most sailors. The men who came to Snug Harbor were, therefore, generally physically debilitated, usually without any financial security and often unfamiliar with the customs of what might be called "polite society."

The eight Trustees named in Randall's will were among New York's most successful leaders—holders of high public office, important figures in the business community, sea captains and clergymen. They were charged with the creation and maintenance of a community composed of men whose values and orientation were of another order; only two of the Trustees were sea-going men. Although the Trustees obviously possessed leadership ability their daily responsibilities were great, and the time they could devote to Snug Harbor severely limited. Furthermore, the short term of those Trustees who were political office-holders—the

Mayor, the Recorder and the Chancellor—made continuity of leadership difficult and contributed to absenteeism at Trustee meetings. In 1835 a petition was submitted to the state legislature to enlarge the board by appointing three additional Trustees. Fearing that these might become politically motivated appointments, however, the Trustees withdrew their request a short time later. In 1846 the board shrank to seven members when the post of Chancellor was ended by an act of the legislature.* Leadership on the Board came to rest primarily with a nucleus of four—the clergy and the representatives of the Marine Society. The clergymen placed great emphasis on the residents' religious and cultural life and were strong advocates of temperance. The Marine Society Trustees promoted the nautical traditions of obedience and correct behavior. Although these interests were not mutually exclusive, the Board was often divided on key issues, and the other Board Members had to align themselves with the opinions expressed either by the "pulpit" or the "cabin."

The Trustees held quarterly meetings, one of them at the institution, and elected a visiting committee for more frequent visits to Staten Island. They appointed a Superintendent to oversee the operation of the institution. With the title of Governor, he was their sole representative and, like the captain of the sailing vessel, was given complete charge of Snug Harbor's institutional life.

John Whetten, a retired sea captain who had sailed in the China trade and was a former president of the Marine Society, became Snug Harbor's first Governor. *The Sailor's Magazine,* A Christian evangelical publication, described Whetten as "one of Neptune's noblest sons." With a sea-going man as chief administrator the nautical tenor of the institution was assured. Under the leadership of Captain Whetten and following a set of "wholesome rules" drawn up by the Trustees to regulate the inmate behavior, life soon fell into routine at Snug Harbor.

Once they arrived at the Harbor the men no longer had to worry about any physical need. The Trustees provided not only food and shelter and the services of nurses and a doctor, but they also provided the residents with their clothing, matrons to care for it and even their tobacco. For those not bed-ridden, the daily routine centered around rising bell, mealtimes and attendance at religious services. The men were permitted to smoke in a common room in the basement or beneath the shade trees in summer. Many would take day-long trips into Manhattan via the ferry, which stopped at the dock three times daily, or make shorter strolls about the island neighborhood. However, idleness soon prompted troublemaking, and after the first year able-bodied men were required to help with the maintenance of the building and farm. For recreation they enjoyed games of dominoes, basket-making or simply sitting, talking or reading. A library was established in 1841 and housed several hundred books selected by the clergy Trustees, and an adjacent reading room held six daily newspapers. Pin alleys and shuffleboards were constructed in 1845.

By 1836 the Trustees' by-laws listed some twenty regulations governing resident behavior. A sampling of the strictures includes the following:

> Any member or subordinate officer of the Institution who shall bring in or cause to be brought into it, any ardent spirits or intoxicating liquors shall be forthwith expelled.
>
> Any member who shall be convicted of getting drunk, either on or off the premises of the Sailors' Snug Harbor, of quarrelling with or assaulting any of his fellow-inmates, or of using profane or obscene language, or of leaving the premises without permission from the Superintendent or one of the assistants, shall forfeit his rights to the benefits of the Institution and shall be expelled from the same.
>
> Every member shall attend all the religious services of the Institution which may be appointed by the Trustees, unless he shall have been excused on account of sickness or of some other sufficient cause.
>
> The inmates of the Institution shall rise at the ringing of the Bell at such hours as the Trustees may direct. They shall take their meals together at the common table and shall be assembled for that purpose by the ringing of the Bell. The Bell to be rung twice at intervals of fifteen minutes immediately preceding each meal.
>
> No person shall commence eating at the table before the blessing shall have been asked; none leave his seat after eating until thanks shall have been returned by some person appointed or called upon to officiate on the occasion.
>
> Members of the Institution are strictly forbidden to indulge in contentious, boisterous or disorderly conversation at the table, and are solemnly enjoined to demean themselves in a decorous manner, becoming of aged and honest seamen.

---

*In 1907 the Board lost another member when the post of Recorder was ended by the city.

There shall be no lights allowed in any part of the building after nine o'clock, excepting the night lamps in the Hall, and it shall be the duty of the assistants to see the lights extinguished accordingly.

The rules indicate that the main concern of the Trustees lay in the area of drunkenness and unruly "sailor-like" behavior. The Trustees hoped to encourage values they considered more appropriate to "aged and honest seamen"—good manners, cleanliness, orderliness and religious devotion.

The drinking problem seemed particularly resistant to the by-laws prohibiting it. For example, in the first few months of Snug Harbor's existence several residents sold the new clothing provided by the Trustees and were found drunk in the Staten Island neighborhood. The problem was not unique to Snug Harbor, of course, and similar difficulties with drunkenness and rules prohibiting it were found at the Naval Asylum in Philadelphia and the Seamen's Retreat in New York.

The problem results in part from the fact that each sailor while at sea was generally given a daily liquor ration of half a pint of rum or whiskey. Later this ration, diluted with water, was called grog. It was believed that the liquor was necessary to support the sailor's strenuous labor. The daily grog ration was firmly entrenched as a part of the U.S. maritime law, but early in the nineteenth century reformers saw its danger. Naval physicians argued that it only promoted a desire for additional liquor. By mid-century, some sailors began to abstain from their grog ration—with the increasing support of the temperance movement—while other sailors and lawmakers fought strongly to keep it as a traditional right. A rebate of six cents per day to those seamen who did not take their ration was designed to encourage abstinence. With the grog ration as an integral part of his life, it is no wonder that the sailor often had a problem of excessive drinking. The grog ration was not legally abolished until 1862.

One reason for locating the Harbor away from Randall's Manhattan farm had been the Trustee's fear that the upper Broadway site in the rapidly growing city would be "exposed to many temptations." "Considering the habits and character of seamen," they wrote in a post-script to the copy of Randall's will, a more quiet setting had been sought for the Snug Harbor.

But even the Staten Island location did not prevent the men from getting liquor. It was clearly the most troublesome problem in the early days of the institution. "There is scarcely a day allowed to pass without more or less indications of intemperance," the *Minutes* of 1836 note. "There have been several instances of individuals having been found beastly drunk upon the road and brought home by strangers to the disgrace of the Institution and mortification of the sober part of its members."

To curb the problem, rules outlawing drunkenness were posted and backed up by the threat of expulsion, but given the freedom of the men to come and go and the availability of liquor near the Harbor the problem persisted. The Governor asked the Presbyterian minister Rev. W. W. Phillips to lecture to the men on the evils of rum drinking, and requested a similar lecture by the Chancellor of the State. "Should these means fail," the Governor reported to the Trustees, "the only alternative will be to erect a wall around the buildings."

Words failed, and construction of a fence was ordered. Lodges were placed at three gates with watchmen controlling traffic in and out of the Institution. In 1842 the wooden fence was replaced by the handsome seven-foot iron fence (Fig. 11) that still encloses the grounds today. In 1847 the Governor, trying to meet the sailor's habit for grog, provided the men with a daily ration of cider. This practice was ended after a short time when it was found that some men traded their cider to local citizens for hard liquor. Neither the fence and the cider nor the stern warnings of the by-laws was successful in preventing drunkenness in some men. Various efforts would be made throughout the next fifty years to deal with the problem.

A second important feature of the by-laws was the emphasis placed on required attendance at religious services. With revivalism sweeping the country in the early nineteenth century, the concern for the spiritual welfare of sailors then is hardly surprising. Bethel Societies, which featured preaching services and encouraged Bible reading among sailors, began to flourish around 1818 with the founding of the Society for Promotion of the Gospel Among Seamen in the Port of New York. The Mariners' Church in New York was opened by the Society in 1820. The American Seamen's Friend Society—created in 1826 as a national effort of all Bethel Societies—broadened its Christian concern for sailors and encouraged the creation of proper boarding houses equipped with libraries and adequate accommodations. They also encouraged the establishment of savings banks for sailors, founded schools for their general education, commissioned missionaries and published tracts especially written for sailors. Although the creation and endowment of Snug Harbor had no direct connection to these societies, the pervasiveness of the movement was reflected there as well.

Religious services were held at the institution from the beginning—morning and evening prayer and Sunday worship in the Presbyterian or Episcopalian tradition—and in 1848 a full-time chaplain was appointed. If the chaplain was absent or ill, the Governor conducted the services. Originally the services were held in the main hall of the central building, but in 1854 work began on a chapel building. On a rainy day in November 1855, the cornerstone of the chapel was laid. Rev. Phillips addressed the crowd of guests and seamen in the large hall, reviewing the history of the founding of Snug Harbor. Then all went in a "great umbrella procession" to position the cornerstone. An elaborate festivity followed in the new dining hall, as this news account reports:

> The old seamen laying up in ordinary at the Snug Harbor, down the Bay, received company yesterday. They had a good time; so did their visitors. There were two hundred men who ventured out in the storm, to eat drink and be jolly with the tars.... A collation was set forth which nobody in these parts had better try to excel. The best of it was that nobody got drunk, the entertainment being wholly temperance. The Mayor presided, and gave a sentiment, "The Memory of Captain Randall."

When the chapel was opened the following fall Phillips preached to the assembled Snugs and important guests, who included the Chancellor of the University of the City of New York and the President of Columbia College. He gave a stirring evangelical interpretation of the chapel as the place for the retired seamen to hear of God's judgment and salvation. In his dramatic conclusion Phillips revealed his philosophy of the institution. Having escaped the ravages and dangers of the sea, he said, the residents have been brought by "beneficent Providence" to this Snug Harbor with its abundant comfortable accommodations. Of the new challenges—of life on shore—he cautioned:

> You are here, however, not to spend your time in idleness, in the mere animal indulgence of eating, and drinking, and sleeping; but you are here to *refit*. Your voyage has not yet terminated; the most important part of it is yet before you; there are quicksands, concealed rocks, whirlpools, and yawning gulphs. There may be a darker, severer, and more terrific storm, and a more awful warring of the elements still in reserve for you, than any through which you have ever passed—you may yet be hopelessly wrecked, and left to sink into the deep and unfathomable abyss. Have you prepared your bark for this last part of your voyage, and are you sure all is right? Are you making daily observations, watching the clouds and the winds, and the tides, and are you habitually ready to launch at any moment? Above all, have you engaged Him who alone can pilot you safely through this dangerous sea into the haven of eternal rest?

Waiting out the last years of their life, Phillips declared, the residents were to use the remainder of their time on shore to refit for the heavenly voyage. Phillips' address was so well received that the Trustees—returning to the city on board the steamboat *Staten Islander*—held a meeting to thank him, and ordered the address prepared for publication.

The chapel's opening service in 1856 may be seen as the high point of the Harbor's early years. It had grown from a single building with thirty-seven men to a large institution housing more than three hundred. These pioneer years were ones of enthusiasm and zeal, epitomized by the fervor of Phillips' sermon and the moralism of the Trustees' by-laws.

Expansion and Controversy (1865-1898)

Rev. Phillips died in March 1865, ending thirty-nine years of outstanding leadership on the Board of Trustees. His death, which coincided with the end of the Civil War, marks the beginning of a new era at the Harbor. There is no evidence that the war interrupted life at the Harbor; the only reference to it in the *Minutes* occurs in September 1863 when construction of a new parsonage was delayed by "the troubled state of the community." However, a post-Civil War era at the Harbor does seem evident. As in our national life, this period at the Harbor was characterized by increasing wealth, rapid growth and troubled leadership.

From 1867 to 1898 Snug Harbor's development was determined in large part by the personalities of two strong-willed Governors. Thomas Melville, brother of *Moby Dick's* great author Herman Melville, became Governor in 1867 and guided the daily life of the institution for seventeen years during its post-war expansion. His governorship was marked by controversy from the start and ended only with his unexpected death at age fifty-six. In the early years the Harbor had been run like a ship with the captain at the helm and tight discipline expected of the crew. To this was added an evangelical concern for the spiritual welfare of the aged seamen. The inadequacies of this approach to an institution now increasing in size and complexity soon became apparent. Events at Snug Harbor during Melville's term and in the fourteen years of his successor, Governor Trask, generated dissensions of such magnitude as to draw public attention.

Melville's appointment as Governor was not unanimous, and one year later, when he was reappointed, the Vice President of the Marine Society objected—saying he "wished with the Marine Society to have a Governor at the head of the Institution, who was an old New York Shipmaster of mature years, and one who would be approved of by that Society, and selected from among its members, and that he was prepared to name such a gentleman." Melville was only thirty-seven, and although he had successfully commanded a clipper ship for seven years he was not from the Marine Society circle. A man of ambition, Melville persisted and successfully defeated the other contenders for the position. He went on to win support from others on the Board of Trustees—including the Marine Society representatives—maintained his post and even survived scandal concerning his use of Harbor funds for personal needs.

In 1872 Melville's former clerk charged him with misusing Harbor supplies and funds. Melville was accused of appropriating the Harbor's food supply (specifically milk, bread and chickens!) for the personal use of his family without reimbursing the Trustees. The Governor defended his actions but the Trustees felt otherwise and instructed him to pay for all such provisions in the future. The investigation produced no direct evidence of embezzlement, but all purchasing was subsequently handed over to a newly created Comptroller's Office set up in Manhattan—independent from the Staten Island institution and Melville's direction.

Although Melville was very well paid in the post of governor he seemed always eager for further advancement. He requested several times, but to no avail, that the Trustees reimburse him for personal expenditures. He enjoyed steady raises and, of course, use of the Governor's house. In 1875 he requested a raise of $1,000, making his salary $4,000. He based his request on the assumption he should receive $1,000 more than the Physician, the next highest ranking employee. Melville apparently thought that his princely tastes were not inconsistent with Snug Harbor's burgeoning wealth.

During Melville's tenure the Harbor enrollment nearly doubled. Rising income from the Manhattan land rentals enabled the Trustees to increase its facilities steadily. In 1876, when the enrollment had reached six hundred, a new dormitory was begun behind the three main buildings; three other dormitories were completed in rapid succession by 1880, enabling the Harbor to house eight hundred residents.

In spite of this expansion Harbor officials were accused of not admitting all the seamen they should. An 1879 letter from the President of the Commission of Public Charities and Correction to the Mayor in his capacity as Trustee complains that the Harbor does not admit as many elderly sailors as they should. And in the same year a letter from the surgeon of the U.S. Marine Hospital Service reports to the Mayor on the "extreme difficulty men experience in gaining admission to the institution; old age, long service at sea, and disability being of little avail, unless supplemented by influence which the managers of the institution regard." He goes on to say that men are denied admission on the technicality that they are not "sailors," having worked on steam vessels or in engine rooms rather than 'before the mast.' It was apparently true, as the surgeon stated, that under the pressure of increasing enrollment men were denied admission to Snug Harbor for this reason. To a similar complaint from another Marine Hospital executive the Trustees passed a resolution asking, in short, that he mind his own business and not meddle in the affairs of Sailors' Snug Harbor.

Although Melville is described by an 1873 visitor as "genial," there is much evidence that he was a strong disciplinarian who was disliked by many residents. Order during Melville's tenure—with its problems of ever-increasing enrollment—was maintained by ever-tighter rules and regulations. In 1867, Melville's first year, the following legalistically worded regulation concerning the work requirement was adopted at the Governor's request:

> All inmates required by the Governor or Steward to work on the farm, garden or grounds of the Sailors' Snug Harbor shall work *five* hours per day for at least *three* days in a week, unless physically unable to do the work required; which fact must be certified to the Governor in writing by the Resident Physician. Any inmate without such certificate, refusing to work when required, shall be 'tabooed' for two months, his tobacco shall be stopped, and he shall not be allowed to make baskets or mats, or to do any work by which he can earn money. Any inmate breaking this 'taboo' shall be forthwith expelled from the Institution.

The word "taboo" first appears during Melville's tenure. It was the punishment for breaking Snug Harbor rules, and consisted of denying certain liberties to the resident. In 1876 when new by-laws were drawn up the following "pledge"—apparently under the influence of the temperance movement—was required of all applicants:

> I, _____, having been received as an inmate of the Sailors' Snug Harbor, do hereby agree to abstain from all intoxicating liquors, and to readily and cheerfully perform such labor and service in and about the Institution and Farm as may be required of me by the Governor, without expecting or claiming any reward or remuneration therefore; also to attend church at least once every Sunday in the Sailors' Snug Harbor Chapel, unless excused by the Governor; also to conduct myself in a quiet, orderly manner, and to strictly obey all the rules and regulations of the Institution.

To enforce the rules and taboos, the Chief Steward and certain residents appointed by him were made monitors and were to report any infractions of the rules to the Governor. One resident referred to the monitors as the "Tweed Ring." In 1879 an anonymous resident produced a book entitled *A History of the Sailors' Snug Harbor Together With Incidents of a Life in it For Eighteen*

Months, in which he tells of the taboo given for drunkenness:

> Should some of the inmates, when walking out be sorely tempted by their appetite for what is more or less common to that class of men, and through the indulgence of it should, upon their arrival at the entrance of the Harbor, 'be struck aback,' or not make a 'clean full pass' through the gate, they are reminded the next morning that their presence at the Governor's office is necessary, when upon arriving before that august personage, they are subjected to three punishments, as it were, in one. They are deprived of their liberty outside the iron fence, deprived of their tobacco, which to some sailors is the next comfort to their 'grog,' and if making baskets or working in any manner for their own benefit, are deprived of that privilege also for that length of time which the Governor may, in his caprice, see fit to bestow upon them. Punishment is expressed by the word 'taboo,' and many are the jokes among the inmates about their being on the 'boo.'

The anonymous author also voices his opinion of Governor Melville: "The writer cannot compliment the Trustees very highly for their wisdom and sagacity in their selection of the local officers." He says very diplomatically, "the prevailing opinion of the inmates, I think, is that his position could be better filled by someone else."

An 1880 letter written to the Mayor by another resident indicates the existence of the Governor's assistants (whom he calls the "Ring") and requests that the Mayor send one of his employees in secret to the Harbor to observe the conditions in the Hospital:

> Dear Sir:
> Send down one of your Clerks on the 11 o'clock A.M. boat or perhaps, 10 o'clock would be better so as to get into the Hospital by 11½ o'clock. He can then see how things are carried on here. Do not let Mr. Snow [the Steward] know anything about this, for he is at the head of the Ring. Men have complained to him about the food and asked for extras, but cannot get them. Dying men cannot eat such coarse food.
>
> Yours truly,
> A Looker On

There is no record of the Mayor's reply, but presumably things did not improve. With increasing numbers of suspensions and expulsions, the matter came to public attention two years later. In September 1882 William Garland, a Snug Harbor resident, addressed a petition to the Mayor requesting a full hearing by the Trustees. He complains:

> Governor Melville treats the inmates in a very cruel and brutal manner. The inmates are so cowed by their treatment that they dare not complain for fear that their treatment may be worse; that the Governor tells any who complain that they are not compelled to remain in the institution, that if they are discontented they can go out.

The request for a hearing was not heeded by the Mayor, so the critics brought their charges to the press. Melville's leadership was criticized in a November 2, 1882, *Nautical Gazette* editorial: "The good and comfortable home which was given and intended as such by the founder, has been converted into a Poor House under prison rules... with officers overbearing and unwarrantable in exercise of their authority."

The editorial was followed by letters to the editor indicating further the nature of the dissatisfaction with Melville's management. A Staten Island neighbor wrote of the strict daily routine which included the "Crockery Brigade," when the old men had to line up in the early morning to empty their chamber pots. A letter from a resident mentions the lack of fruit in his menu. "He can look through the fence at the governor's and steward's gardens, and that is all he will get of the apples, pears, peaches and grapes that are growing there." Another complains of Sunday church attendance: "As the Governor's carriage, on Sunday morning, rolls off with his household to worship in the manner that best suits their convenience, conscience or clothes, the seven hundred inmates are obliged to follow the gravelled channel that leads to the Church of the Holy Snugs." Although Roman Catholic residents were allowed to attend churches in the neighborhood, those men who did not attend the Protestant services at the Snug Harbor Church were denied smoking privileges and required to remain quietly in their rooms.

A resident who left the Harbor after six months wrote the Mayor saying the Governor was "cruel and barbarous." He charges that Melville refused to return to him the money entrusted by his sister for his care. These fairly numerous complaints, although to be expected in an institution with so many men, suggest that Melville was less than sympathetic to the wishes of the residents.

In December, further complaints were addressed to the Trustees and a full hearing was soon instituted. A panel of five men conducted week-long hearings and in February 1883 issued a statement finding the complaints without merit. Petitioner William Garland, and another resident who wrote a critical newspaper article, with a third resident, were dismissed from the institution.

Despite Melville's troubles with the residents he seems to have been greatly admired in his family circle and particularly by his brother Herman. His household in the Governor's Residence included an unmarried sister, his aging mother, until her death in 1871, and many relatives who visited for varying lengths of time. Although Thomas Melville and his wife, Elizabeth Bogert, daughter of the Resident Physician, had no children of their own, the house was often filled with the Melville clan. Herman wrote to a friend in 1877, "Last evening I went down to the Island and anchored for the night in the Snug Harbor." This documents only one of many visits by Herman, who considered his brother his closest friend. (Melville enthusiasts will recall that Herman dedicated his first novel, *Redburn,* to his brother.) Herman reveals his great admiration for his brother in a letter to an uncle about the Christmas dinner Thomas hosted at Snug Harbor: It was a "bountiful and luxurious banquet...a big table belted round by big appetites and bigger hearts, but the biggest of all the hearts was at the head table—being big with satisfaction at seeing us enjoying ourselves."* This description provides a poignant contrast to the conditions suggested by the residents' complaints. Melville's generosity was not a part of the Governor seen by them.

If Herman Melville was aware of any dissatisfaction with his brother's leadership, he mentions it in neither his writing nor his correspondence. He does refer, however, to a wholly pleasant episode, in an April 13, 1877, letter to Evert Duyckinck, the New York Literary figure. Herman mentions Duyckinck's gift to the Harbor of four pictures depicting the Battle of the Nile. Melville apparently encouraged Duyckinck in selecting these pictures and choosing a spot for their display, "where the old salts can look up at them from off their dominoes. All you have to do, is provide for an annual lecture to be delivered before the old veterans in the big hall of the Institution, on the Battle of the Nile, the pictures serving to illustrate the matter." The pictures are still in Snug Harbor's collection and, although badly faded, are an interesting legacy from the Melville era.

Thomas Melville's death in March 1884 was unexpected, as an obituary in the *Nautical Gazette* makes clear:

> Captain Thomas Melville, the Governor of Sailors' Snug Harbor, died suddenly of heart disease on Wednesday night (5th inst.). The deceased reached his residence at the Harbor at 8 o'clock, and was apparently in the best of health. Soon afterwards he complained of a suffocating sensation and died three hours later. He was 55 years old.

A eulogy in the *Minutes* of March 29 speaks of Melville's leadership and notes that he enriched the beauty of the Harbor; it discreetly avoids mention of his troubles. During his tenure four major dormitories had been constructed, the iron fence extended, the two gatehouses built, the church tower added, the main hall of the center building redecorated as it appears today and a statue of Randall commissioned from Augustus Saint-Gaudens. Much of the beauty of today's Snug Harbor was indeed created in Melville's time.

Although another controversy was developing during Melville's years, it did not then come to public attention. The Snug Harbor residents had fallen into the regular practice of selling their votes in the political elections! Melville's successor G. D. S. Trask, a former sea captain who had sailed between New York and Liverpool, was ordered by the Trustees to end this custom. "For 25 years or more," the Trustees said in a report on the matter, "The Snug Harbor has been made an open market for the buying and selling of votes at local, state, and national elections." The Trustees realized that the presence of so large a number of purchasable votes was sufficient to debase the local political process and might often be enough to tip the scales in local and state elections, and were determined to take vigorous steps "to root out the evil."

Governor Trask posted notice prior to the November 1884 election (the first election after Melville's death) that any resident convicted of taking money for his vote would be expelled. Many were convicted and the expulsions of residents caused much ill will, but the selling apparently continued. A full investigation of the voting practices was not conducted for another five years.

---

*Information about the Melville family and Herman's interest in Staten Island is found in "Melville's Staten Island 'Paradise,'" by J. J. Boies, *Staten Island Historian,* Vol. 27, July-September 1966, pp. 24-28.

During several days of hearings in 1889, well over five hundred residents gave testimony. The following statement reveals the extent of the problem.

> "First—That money has been paid to the inmates of Sailors' Snug Harbor at nearly all elections in the Harbor, for many years.
>
> Second—That previous to November 1884, money was openly paid for votes by politicians who carried leather bags containing green backs and silver which they distributed to inmates outside and inside the grounds of the Harbor, and in some cases within the walls of the Institution itself. And most if not all of the recipients knew and understood that the money they received was for the vote they had cast in the interst of certain individuals or parties.
>
> Third—That since November, 1884, when Captain G. D. S. Trask, the present Governor, issued notices and conspicuously posted the same in and around the Institution notifying inmates that receipt of pay of any description for their vote, would be regarded as sufficient justification for their 'expulsion from the Institution,' politicians, sometimes aided by certain inmates who were workers for the respective parties, have adopted a form of ticket or token which has been given to certain inmates who in return, got it redeemed either at some saloon, in the neighborhood or by and through a friendly inmate well known to the politicians and in some cases acting for and in concert with them.

After Trask's pronouncement of 1884, as the statement indicates, tokens were substituted for cash and redeemed at Peter McHugh's bar opposite the Snug Harbor Railway Station. Over half of the men examined in the investigation admitted having received payment for their votes—one dollar for local elections and two dollars for presidential elections. Some of the residents were "workers" who induced others to go to the polls and told them how to vote; they were paid five to ten dollars per day. The investigation report indicted one agile and powerful resident, David Sherry, as the key worker from whom the men received their tokens:

> At the February election he [Sherry] not only hoodwinked his party, but in numerous cases he knowingly palmed upon ignorant voters a certain ticket, when he knew they intended to vote the opposite ticket, and although it is not stated directly...he had stipulated a few hours before the election to hand over the whole Institution vote to one political party for a sum simply because the other party would not come up to his and his co-workers' financial expectations.

The investigation revealed the full extent of these practices and provoked anger among the residents, particularly the friends of those expelled. In November 1890 a resident named Anderson fired three shots at Trask. The Governor was not wounded, but Pinkerton Guards were now assigned to protect him and maintain order at the next election.*

The election scandal aside, Governor Trask was deeply involved with the new building program at the Harbor begun in 1890. An 1898 bird's-eye view of the Harbor reveals that the prosperity evident in the embellishments and building programs of the Melville era was continued during the fourteen years of Trask's governorship. (Figs. 12, 13.) Although enrollment did not increase as dramatically during these years it did continue to rise, and new, more elaborate accommodations were added. In 1890, with the annual surplus reaching $100,000, the Trustees decided to construct an "Amusement Hall" (unimagined in Phillips' "refitting" program of 1856) as well as a new, more impressive church building.

The location of the 1890s buildings was determined by the new means of approach to the Harbor. The principal access was now the shore road, which approached the main buildings from the east, rather than the road from the dock, because the Staten Island Transit Rail Road line and a street car line now linked the Harbor with new ferry terminals in that direction. With the eastern side of the property more prominent, architect Robert Gibson decided to accept the Trustees' suggestion of locating the new buildings there, despite the consequent reshuffling of existing buildings.

The white marble church with its portico, Renaissance dome and towers reflects the Beaux Arts style then gaining popularity in American architecture. It

---

*The problem of the residents' voting privileges did not end with the Trask era. In 1903 the right to vote was taken from the residents when the court declared that New York law did not permit "wards of charities" to vote. This ruling held until 1946, when two residents of the Harbor challenged it and the voting privilege was restored.

was dedicated on April 5, 1893, and named the Randall Memorial Church. It seated only two hundred seventy—less than the entire Harbor population—as attendance at religious services was no longer compulsory.

The Music Hall similar to the church in style, could seat six hundred and became the Harbor's center of entertainment. The architecture was described as "splendid" when Staten Island neighbors attended a December 1893 concert. Governor Trask was congratulated on the fine entertainment he offered the residents.

A circular pool with fountains and a statue of Neptune was installed in front of the buildings in 1895, completing the new arrangement of the eastern side. Meanwhile, on the western side of the compound the Sanitorium—an enormous X-shaped building whose intersecting wings provided light and fresh air across each ward—was begun in 1897.

It was also during Trask's tenure that the Harbor acquired its important collection of marine paintings. *The Century Magazine* in 1884 mentions his interest in art, saying he was responsible for an "old master" reproduction being in every room. A picture committee appointed by the Trustees commissioned T. W. Wood in 1894 to copy Trumball's full-length portrait of Alexander Hamilton. Trask's portrait by Thomas P. Anschutz later joined the collection, along with several marine paintings owned by Trask, bringing the total to more than a hundred paintings.

Trask, like Melville, was a strict disciplinarian. He was disliked by many of the men and some urged his resignation. His discipline allowed little sympathy for individual residents, and, he sometimes displayed a temper. A visitor to the Marine Society meeting described Trask's response to criticism of Snug Harbor —"His face was full of contortions, livid with rage...he was loudly pounding the table with his clenched fist." The vice president of the Marine Society came to Trask's aid in 1897, defending his discipline. He said the trouble with the Harbor is created by the "mixed sailors" (not all were officers of ships), "some of whom are first class merchantmen, but others are 'pirates,'" the latter having created the "mutinous condition" in attempting to oust Trask. "My colleagues may not agree with me, but I am thoroughly convinced, that no man other than a ship master and a thorough disciplinarian can manage the Sailors' Snug Harbor in view of the wicked element that gets in it from time to time."

We do not know the details of what happened in 1898 to finally force Trask's retirement. A hand written note in a Marine Society Memorium reads: "Captain Trask was in trouble at the Sailors' Snug Harbor, and was given the choice of resigning or being fired. He resigned." The lengthy eulogy published by the Society in 1913 makes no mention of the fourteen years he served as Snug Harbor Governor.

Trask's resignation in 1898 marks the end of another era at Snug Harbor. Both Trask and Melville presided during a time of unprecedented growth and change. The public notoriety that had characterized their era at the Harbor was soon forgotten, leaving the Harbor to enjoy several decades of peace and quiet.

Halcyon Years (1899-1940)

With the resident population stabilized at approximately nine-hundred fifty and the major building programs completed, the turn of the century ushered in Snug Harbor's most tranquil years. The 1898 bird's-eye view (Fig. 12) gives an idea of the elegant, self-sufficient world the Harbor presented. With its magnificent buildings surrounded by gravelled walks and flower-bordered lawns it presented the atmosphere of a grand resort. A description of this self-contained world accompanying the 1898 illustration in *Leslie's Weekly* speaks of the Harbor as "the haughtiest and richest charitable institution in the world." One of the residents is quoted as saying "We are rich, enormously rich, independently rich. We don't know how rich we are. It ain't the Trustees' money, it ain't the city's money, it's our money—Captain Randall's money. We ain't beholden to anybody outside the Harbor, and we don't want them."

Presiding over the affluent Harbor of the early 1900s was Governor Daniel Delahanty, who received the post as Trask's successor. Delahanty was a Commander in the U.S. Navy and the first naval captain to receive the governorship, the Harbor having been headed always by a mercantile captain. Delahanty served as Governor while on shore leave from the Navy, and shortly after his appointment in 1898 was called back for six months' active duty during the Spanish-American War. He became a hero as captain of the *Sewanee,* which ran the blockade before the forts of Santiago Harbor. Upon his triumphal return, Delahanty received a memorial sword from the Secretary of the Navy which, according to a news account, brought forth a "roar of delight from the throats of the 600 white-haired seadogs" gathered in the Snug Harbor Music Hall for the ceremony.

The tranquillity of Delahanty's tenure was interrupted briefly in the fall of 1899 when a Snug Harbor physician and several nurses brought charges against him concerning his conduct in the Hospital. A Dr. Joy complained that Delahanty, wearing heavy boots and speaking loudly, visited the men late at night and required too strict discipline of the nurses. After several days of testimony both for and against the Governor no action was taken by the Trustees. The *New York Times* reported that no evidence of improper behavior was revealed; the charges displayed only the "petty jealousies" existing at the institution. The two Marine Society Trustees who had championed Trask and opposed Delahanty's appointment were apparently eager to find fault with the Navy Commander and anxious to have the leadership back in the hands of a merchant-marine man.

Trask, after his retirement from the Governor's

post, had been elected president of the Marine Society and therefore a Trustee of Snug Harbor. In December 1900 he refused renomination to the Board, stating he found himself at variance with other members and with its management. The *Times* reported him as saying "Our chief difference of opinion arises from the fact that they are inclined to give preference to old sailors of the U.S. Navy in conferring the benefits of the institution," adding that Randall had wanted the Snug Harbor to be the home of merchant seamen. But Trask's comments were a minor disruption, and Delahanty served ten years without further public notice.

On May 28, 1902, the Harbor celebrated the hundredth anniversary of its founding. Although the ceremonies were described as "modest," they were an opportunity for the Harbor to display its great wealth. Over one thousand formal invitations, printed by Tiffany's, were sent out. Eight hundred guests arrived from Manhattan on the steamboat *Valley Girl,* which had been chartered for the occasion, and the Tug *Nina* brought officers from the Brooklyn Navy Yard. In all, two thousand celebrants were present. Arriving at noon the guests were first given a tour of the flag-draped main building, then treated to an organ concert at the Randall Memorial Church and a visit to the Hospital and the newly completed Sanitorium. A champagne luncheon was served in tents on the Hospital lawn, to the accompaniment of music by the Mt. Loretto Boy's Band. After lunch a vaudeville entertainment was held beside the Governor's mansion. A copy of the *Social Register,* as noted on Tiffany's bill, may have helped the Governor's private secretary with the guest list. Among the dignitaries attending were the Secretary of State of New Jersey, a supreme Court Judge, and all but one of the Harbor Trustees.

The wealth of the Harbor was now legendary, and attracted the sarcasm of early twentieth-century journalists. A 1908 article in the *Independent,* a weekly news magazine, commented:

> Were the sailors to breakfast on plovers' eggs, and terrapin, lunch on pâté de foie gras, and dine on canvas-back duck, with dry champagne and sparkling burgundy thrown in, and if they were to smoke the most expensive cigars and dress in silk and broadcloth, they could not spend a quarter of the income of the estate.

Although hardly the luxurious life suggested by the journalists, the daily schedule of the residents represented a significant departure from the rigors imposed by the nineteenth-century by-laws. During Delahanty's tenure Theodore Dreiser visited the Harbor in 1904 and described the average resident's day:

> Each sailor is permitted to rise when he pleases, though the bell rings at six and breakfast is served at seven, and if he does not get any it is no one's fault but his own. Coffee and crackers are served at three, and supper at six. There is a rule that all shall be in at nine, but this is easily avoided by giving notice at the office that this hour is not to be observed, which ends the matter.
>
> No one is obliged to come or go except as he chooses, and this in addition to the munificence of bed, light, food, clothing, tobacco, newspapers and theatrical entertainment. Only drunkenness and other disagreeable vices of men are punished, and those with good cause.

The old by-laws were dropped and a new booklet entitled "Rules and Information" was issued to each resident in 1922. Some regulations from the earlier by-laws appear but the overall tone is more positive, listing as many conveniences as restrictions. The booklet begins: "All persons admitted to the Institution are on a footing of equality, being entitled to the same privileges and subject to the same duties and obligations." It may be that the present-day custom of addressing all the residents as "Captain," regardless of previous rank, began at this time.

The new liberality is further indicated by information the Trustees provided in a broadside advertising the Harbor in 1933:

> The fullest liberty is allowed the inmates consistent with good order and a due regard for the peace and comfort of the community. It is the intention of the Board of Trustees that the institution shall be a home where our worn-out and disabled sailors may spend their declining years in peace, comfort and self-respect, and it is the aim of its officials to faithfully carry out this intention. The institution is the heritage of the present and future generations of American sailors and it is faithfully managed as such by the Board of Trustees.

During this period at the Harbor one of the Governors, Captain George Beckwith, must have appreciated the changes that had occurred in sea-going

Main Hall, 1975

life and encouraged the older residents to write down their reminiscences of days under sail. Three books written by residents of the Harbor were published during Beckwith's tenure. Frank Waters, a resident who was born around 1855 and began his sailing career at age fourteen aboard clipper ships, wrote a book of tales and poems of his sea-going adventures entitled *Eight Bells — Sailors' Snug Harbor Yarns and Ballads.* He dedicated it to Captain Beckwith, "a gentleman and true Sailors' Friend."

Another resident, also a veteran of clippers and clearly prejudiced against steam-driven vessels, wrote a collection of tales entitled *When Ships Were Ships and Not Tin Pots, the Seafaring Adventures of Captain William Morris Barnes,* which was published in 1930. W. O. Hicks wrote *Sea Tales From Sailors' Snug Harbor* in 1935, which is a collection of tales by Hicks and other men of the Harbor and also includes a guide to the Harbor buildings. It too is dedicated to Beckwith, "my good friend and shipmate."

Prosperity for the institution continued throughout the 1920s and 1930s. In 1922 The *New York Times* called Snug Harbor, with its two million dollar surplus, the richest charitable institution in New York. The *New York Herald Tribune* featured an article on Snug Harbor in 1924 entitled "The Best Paying Farm in the United States," referring to Snug Harbor's Manhattan property. In 1929 the Trustees' Annual Statement to the Common Council of the City of New York reported annual ground rentals from the Washington Square property and other income at $1,340,324; total expenses were $1,035,744, and the reserves gradually accumulated since 1900 amounted to $4,142,224. The enrollment and expenses had remained steady from 1890 into the 1930s, but beyond that date the secure financial position of Snug Harbor—with its seemingly endless flow of money—began to change. The Harbor now entered a new stage in its development.

Modernization and Retrenchment (1941-1976)

The waning years of the Depression saw a gradual erosion of Snug Harbor's earlier affluence. By 1945 the enrollment (three-hundred seventy-five) was half what it had been ten years earlier. The decline can be attributed in part to the independence offered retired sailors by pension plans and Social Security benefits. A gradual decrease in the numbers serving as U.S. Merchant Seamen was also a factor.

By 1940 the Harbor officials realized that the days of large surplus income were over. They now endeavored to revamp the style of operation inherited from the nineteenth century. Funds for maintaining the institution had always come from rental of the Manhattan real estate, or from investments of this income. Throughout the nineteenth century the fashionable Washington Square address had assured a steadily rising income. But in the 1930s and 1940s the city's changing patterns of growth—and a gradual lessening in the quality of the Washington Square buildings themselves—caused the property to decline in rental value. The Trustees modernized some of the buildings, notably the Washington Mews apartments and a section of the houses facing Washington Square, but a war-time construction freeze limited their efforts.

The precise value of the Harbor's land holdings in Manhattan had been subject to speculation from the earliest days. Some writers reported estimates from twenty to forty million dollars. (The Trustees did not include the value of the land in their annual reports, but with the rising financial uncertainties of the post-war era the President of the Board of Trustees would give the land's estimated worth in 1954 as twelve million dollars and generating an annual income of only $500,000.) Not wanting to effect costly modernization by using the Harbor's capital funds—because they were needed for the Staten Island institution itself—the Trustees turned to offering long-term leases under which the tenant would bear the cost of erecting more modern buildings. This practice was begun in 1949, when the whole Washington Square North block was leased to New York University with total options for more than two hundred years. But it was soon apparent that the advantages of these long-term leases, while achieving administrative economies, did not compensate for the effects of post-war inflation.

Burdened by ever-increasing costs, the Trustees also proposed in 1949 to charge a fee to the residents of Snug Harbor. A study of seventy New York institutions for care of the aged, they reported, disclosed that all made use of some type of fee. With income from pension plans and

Social Security, the Trustees found, more and more of their applicants were able to contribute toward their maintenance. Although the financially indigent would not be denied admission, the proposed plan involved a maximum charge of four dollars per day for those able to pay. The more radical feature of the plan called for residents to turn over their assets to the Trustees, and the monthly charges would be drawn from them. Some of the men refused to accept the plan and requested the Attorney General of the State of New York to issue an injunction against the Trustees expelling anyone who refused to pay or sign over his assets.

The 1949 fee plan was the first public indication that Snug Harbor was facing financial difficulties. It was received with utter disbelief by a public knowing only of Snug Harbor's legendary wealth. Mayor O'Dwyer protested the plan. Calling Snug Harbor a "big business," he asked to be relieved of his duties as Trustee. He attended only one meeting of the Board and was granted court permission to withdraw. After a hearing conducted by the Attorney General's office the fee plan was dropped, and the Trustees agreed to an audit of the Harbor's accounts and a survey of its management methods. The audit was completed in five months, but no conclusions were reached nor were changes forthcoming. The Trustees were given the right to reinstate the fee plan in the future if it were approved by the State Supreme Court.

Despite the setback in the fee proposal in 1950 the Trustees now turned to a much-needed task. With the security of long-term leases and some remaining surplus funds, they embarked upon a program to modernize the Staten Island physical plant. Because of fixed income and rising costs, they realized, the institution could provide for only the reduced enrollment. Many buildings were no longer used and some would have to be closed. The first hint of this decision reached the public in July 1950, when the *Staten Island Advance* reported the modernization plans. A dormitory would be converted into a modern Infirmary. The enormous nineteenth-century Hospital and Sanitorium would be abandoned. Three vacant buildings, the cattle barn (the dairy herd had been sold in 1949), a machine shop and carpenter's shop were demolished in June 1951. In July, the three hospital buildings were razed.

The demolition caused little concern in the Staten Island community, but attention soon focused on one of the remaining vacant buildings—the Randall Memorial Church. Its Renaissance dome and twin towers had long been a Staten Island landmark. The Trustees' survey estimated repairs at $56,000.

Staten Island Borough President Cornelius Hall had anticipated the demolition of the building and began discussions with the Trustees concerning its preservation, but to no avail. Borough President Hall felt that the Harbor's long-term tax exemption obliged them to preserve the landmark, but the Trustees remained firm: "While the Trustees would be sympathetic to any proposal for benefit of Staten Island their first consideration must be the welfare of the Mariners." The Borough President proposed using the Church as a concert hall and acquiring the three-and-a-half acres surrounding it as a site for a new building for the Staten Island Museum. The Trustees refused to sell the land but offered the city a dollar-a-year lease for the building for fifty years. The matter went back and forth and ended in condemnation proceedings and renovation for-public-use plans in 1952. Later, however, a twenty-eight million dollar cut in the city's proposed budget left out the Harbor project. At this point, two years after beginning the fight, Borough President Hall abandoned his attempts to save the Randall Memorial Church.

One last effort in the spring of 1952 to save the building was made by a Staten Island citizen, William Lynn McCracken, who appealed to the Episcopal Diocese to preserve it as a retreat center. Conducting an intense campaign McCracken appealed to the church leaders and even Cecil B. DeMille for support of his project, but no help was forthcoming and the demolition crews, who had been standing by for several months, began their work. By September not a stone remained.

With the physical plant trimmed and a former dormitory remodeled as the Infirmary at a cost of one million dollars, the Harbor turned its attention to changing the nature of its institutional life. In 1953 they hired Community Research Associates, Inc., to study their practices with a view to incorporating recent developments in health care for the elderly. Accordingly, the Harbor employed a Deputy Governor with social-services hospital experience, an Occupational Therapist and in 1955, a Social Director. A boost in morale was meanwhile provided in December 1955 when the Ford Foundation awarded the Harbor $38,500 for use in its Infirmary. Research Associates further recommended that financially independent residents be charged a fee, and that the post of Governor be filled by a person specifically trained in institutional care of the aged. The Trustees indicated that income from the trust was not sufficient to support all the changes recommended by

Research Associates; one of the more far-reaching of which was to create an all-new facility on the site or elsewhere.

A management survey was undertaken—in 1958—with an eye to greater economies and improvement in management practices. This study also recommended that the traditional Governor's post be terminated and a Superintendent experienced in hospital care be appointed. It further recommended that the Snug Harbor Comptroller's Office in Manhattan be closed and that a Business Manager be stationed at the Staten Island site. The Marine Society made known their opposition to having a non-maritime man at the head of the Harbor. The Board was deadlocked over this matter in 1959, with the clergy Trustees apparently in favor and the Marine Society Trustees opposed. The tie was broken when the Chamber of Commerce Trustee voted in favor of having a maritime man head the institution.

The 1958 survey may have recommended the sale of some of the Staten Island land as a means of lowering costs and gaining income, because in 1960 the Trustees announced their intention to sell a large tract near the western edge of the property to an apartment developer. The sale did not go through, however, and the tract was landscaped into its present park-like setting in 1967. The Staten Island holdings at that time consisted of approximately eighty acres, the southern block of the original farm having been sold in the 1930s as the suburban development Randall Manor.

In 1965 the Harbor announced a comprehensive plan for modernization. Encouraged by rising national interest in care of the aging, anticipating that income would be raised through fees, and with the prospect of selling part of its Staten Island acreage along Henderson Avenue, the Trustees announced a proposal to create a new, enlarged institution. The plan involved greater independence for the residents with two-and three-room apartments for married residents, as well as a four-story nursing-home. To implement the plan a "complete modernization of the interior of the old buildings" would be necessary.

Edward Noakes & Associates, a Washington, D.C., architectural firm, made a study of the Harbor and in 1965 presented a proposal for the new facilities. Their design involved retaining only the original 1833 Greek Revival building and the 1854 Chapel. All other buildings would be demolished to make way for clustered apartments and high rise buildings. Although the Noakes plan was not made public until 1966, the newly created New York City Landmarks Commission had become aware of the demolition plans in 1965 and proposed landmark designation for the row of five Greek Revival buildings and the Chapel.

Designation of the six buildings was discussed at the first public hearing of the Commission on September 21, 1965. Representing the Trustees at the hearing, Edward H. Noakes described the buildings as obsolete and a hindrance to the purposes of the charity. Henry Hope Reed, of the Museum of the City of New York, long an advocate of preserving New York's historic architecture, spoke of the artistic importance of the buildings. The Board of Estimate approved the landmark status for the Harbor buildings. The Trustees protested the designation, however, and in May 1967 it was overruled by State Supreme Court Justice Charles G. Tierney, who stated that the designation imposed too heavy a burden upon the institution. "The cost of preservation cannot be thrust upon the land owner," the Justice said.

A few months later round three began. The Municipal Arts Society, supported by nineteen other groups including the American Institute of Architects and the Victorian Society of America, with the guidance of Landmarks Preservation Commissioner Terence Benbow, then appealed on behalf of the Landmarks Commission, and in March 1968 Justice Aaron Steuer ruled that further testimony was necessary if the land-marking were to be overturned. Justice Steuer found the buildings to be a valuable part of the national heritage and that it was uncertain whether maintenance of them would interfere with Snug Harbor's charitable purposes.

As the situation seemed to be at an impasse, in 1970 the Trustees proposed constructing a separate all-new facility for one-hundred twenty men on ten acres, and selling the remaining property to finance the new building. (An alternative plan to adapt the landmarked structures as housing for the one-hundred twenty residents had also been prepared by Harbor architects, but it was not approved by the New York State Department of Health or by the Landmarks Commission.) The Trustees simultaneously began to consider a new out-of-state location, and in February 1971 announced plans to move to Sea Level, North Carolina, and formally requested permission from the Surrogate Court to do so. The location was selected because the Daniel Taylor family, pioneers in ocean shipping and railroading between the United States and Cuba, had made an attractive offer of land to the institution. In addition, the Harbor and Duke University's geriatrics hospital—which is located two hundred miles from the new site—had worked out a mutually helpful agreement.

With the move to North Carolina confirmed, in March 1972 the Harbor sold thirteen acres of their Staten Island land, including the principal buildings, to the City of New York and agreed not to pursue further the legality of the landmark designation. The purchase by the city was made possible, in part, because the Staten Island Institute of Arts and Sciences and its Museum relinquished the capital budget allocated for its new museum and applied the funds to the purchase of the Harbor property. The remaining sixty-two acres of the Harbor were sold to an apartment developer for $6.2 million. Strong community opposition to high-density housing on the property—and much skillful lobbying on the part of Staten Island citizens—finally resulted in the announcement made by Mayor Lindsay and Borough President Connor on June 18, 1973, that the city would acquire the remaining sixty-two acres from the developer and mark it as parkland. The Mayor described the Harbor property "as an integral part of the community and neighborhood landscape for more than a hundred years. The site, which commands a spectacular view of New York Bay and the Lower Manhattan skyline, forms a setting of great delight and serenity. It is irreplacable—and losing it unthinkable."

When the move to North Carolina began in 1976, the view of the Harbor from the shore road was a bleak one. Beyond the iron fence two dormitories stood dark and empty. The Music Hall to the rear was roped off, as a warning against plaster falling from the gaping hole in its roof. Along the river, only pilings marked the spot of the once-busy dock. A sign on the gatehouse read "Official Business Only," a warning that visitors were not entirely welcome. Inside the gate, the tall monument to Robert Richard Randall stood as it did on the summer day in 1834, when the Harbor's first residents reinterred his bones there. Past the row of columned buildings and the ancient chestnut trees which once provided a vista for the Hospital, beyond the statue of Randall, the open lawn and flower beds provided a colorful reminder of the more cheerful atmosphere of earlier days.

Despite the losses, Snug Harbor's remaining buildings are a rich treasure of nineteenth-century architecture for New Yorkers to enjoy. Plans are underway to reuse the Harbor's buildings and spacious grounds as a cultural center. Despite the financial crises of the city, Staten Islanders remain hopeful.

The weather vane atop the dome of Snug Harbor's main building—its oldest—turns with the winds as it has done for over one-hundred forty years. As it moves, it creates in the interior of the dome a faint sound reminiscent of the sea and the sea-going adventures of the residents. It has witnessed pioneer days of formation, decades of rapid growth and controversy, mellow years of wealth and ease, and times of declining enrollments and shrinking funds. Snug Harbor is a unique institution that has cared for more then ten thousand men of the sea.

The will of the eighteenth-century gentleman who directed that his wealth be used to establish a Snug Harbor for "aged, decrepit and worn-out sailors" is still being carried out. Attention turns now to North Carolina, where the Harbor has started afresh. The next chapters of the Snug Harbor story will take place there.

Sailor's Snug Harbor, 1853

Part II
Snug Harbor
Album

1. Map of Manhattan Island, 1777
Bordering on Peter Stuyvesant's "Bouwerie," the boundaries of Thomas Randall's Manhattan farm were originally staked out under Dutch grants of 1661 and 1664. During English control the farm was acquired by Lieutenant Governor Andrew Elliot, whose ownership is indicated on this map of 1777. He named it "Minto Farm" in honor of his distant relative, a Scottish Earl and built his residence facing Bowery Lane. Later Frederick Poelintz bought the farm and used it to conduct agricultural experiments. Randall's father purchased the farm from Poelintz in 1790 and Robert inherited it a few years later.

2. Manhattan Island and the Harbor, 1794

Although no contemporary view of the Randall farm exists, a 1794 depiction of the country estate of one of his neighbors suggests how the rolling hills, farms and marshlands in that area of Manhattan once appeared. Shown are the East River, New York Harbor, and on the right, the northward encroaching city in the far distance.

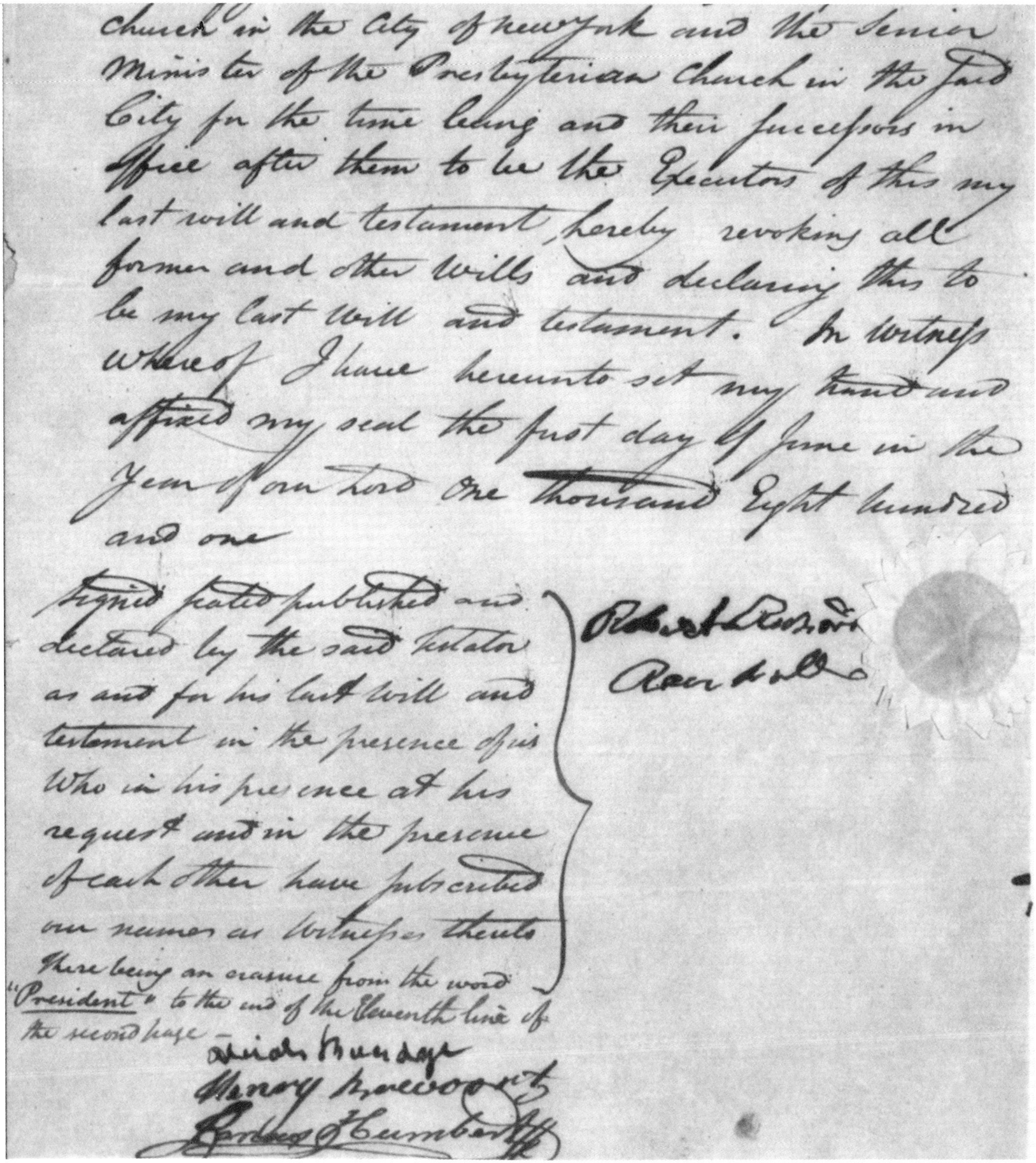

Church in the City of New York and the Senior Minister of the Presbyterian Church in the said City for the time being and their successors in office after them to be the Executors of this my last Will and testament, hereby revoking all former and other Wills and declaring this to be my last Will and testament. In Witness whereof I have hereunto set my hand and affixed my seal the first day of June in the Year of our Lord One thousand Eight hundred and one

Signed sealed published and declared by the said Testator as and for his last Will and testament in the presence of us Who in his presence at his request and in the presence of each other have subscribed our names as witnesses thereto there being an erasure from the word "President" to the end of the Eleventh line of the second page —

Robert Richard Randall

Hugh Mercer
Henry Brockholst
Barnes H—

3. Last Will and Testament of Robert Richard Randall, 1801

4. Map of the Trustees' Property, 1801
City streets and building lots have already been staked out on this property plan made in the year of Randall's death. The northern part of the farm with mansion and orchards was apparently being reserved for use of the institution.

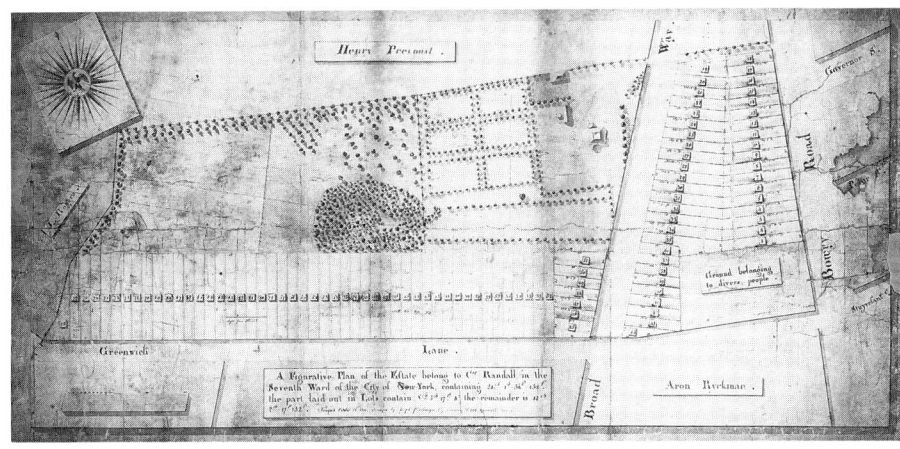

5. Trustees' Seal
The Trustees began the work of founding the institution five years after Randall's death. Incorporating in 1806, they ordered that a seal of the institution be made to depict:

> A secure and tranquil Harbour formed by two points of Land projecting into the Ocean. In this Harbour a ship which appears to have been injured by tempestuous weather is seen riding safely at anchor. On the shore is presented a View of the building erected for accommodation of infirm and decayed seamen. The motto is "Portum petimus fessi," signifying that those who were disabled by the toils and dangers of the Sea have, at last, found a place of rest and safety.

The artist who made the seal, a man identified only as "Robertson," shows an imaginary asylum and ship set in a mountainous landscape.

6. Map of New York City, 1827
The city's rapid growth northward, apparent on this map of 1827, caused the Trustees to consider an alternative site for the Snug Harbor.

7. Map of the Trustees' Property, 1830
An 1830 survey of the farm shows the final arrangement of streets and lots laid out for leasing. The southern boundary of the farm bordered on the newly created Washington Square and its western boundary became Fifth Avenue. Their imminent development as fashionable residential streets added to the fact that Broadway was extended through the middle of the property assured the Trustees of a steady demand for leases.

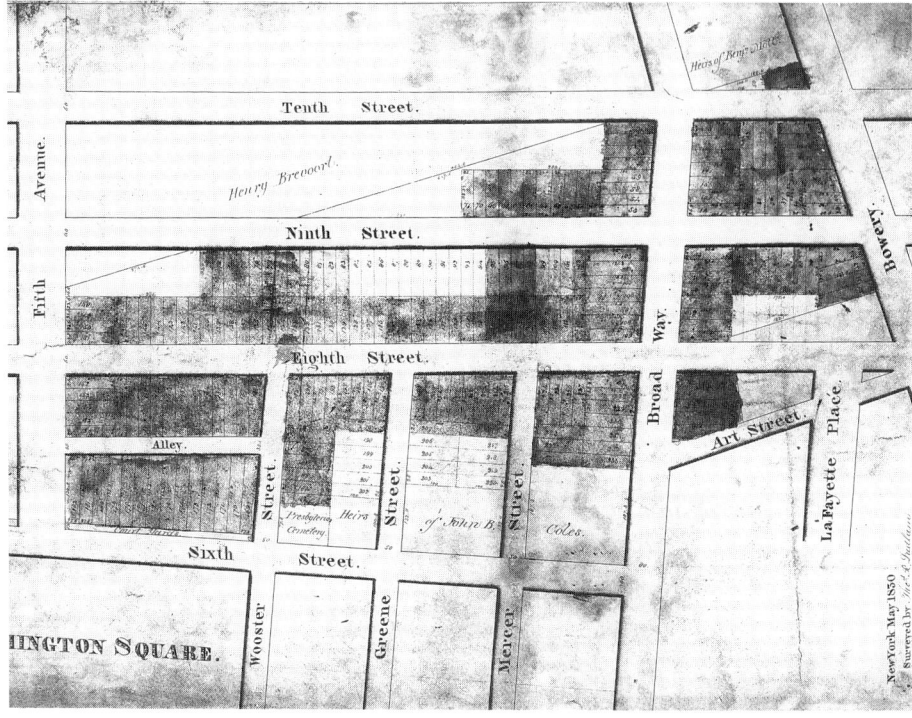

8. 15 Washington Square North
The lots along Washington Square North were leased to wealthy individuals who constructed elegant Greek Revival style townhouses.

9. A. T. Stewart's Store, 1869
The lots on the east side of Broadway between Ninth and Tenth Streets were leased by A. T. Stewart who constructed there in 1861 the city's largest department store.

10. Washington Square, c.1940
Washington Square continued as an elegant address into the twentieth century. One Fifth Avenue, a luxury apartment tower, was built on Trustees' land in 1929. One journalist referred to the Snug Harbor's Manhattan properties as "the best paying farm in America."

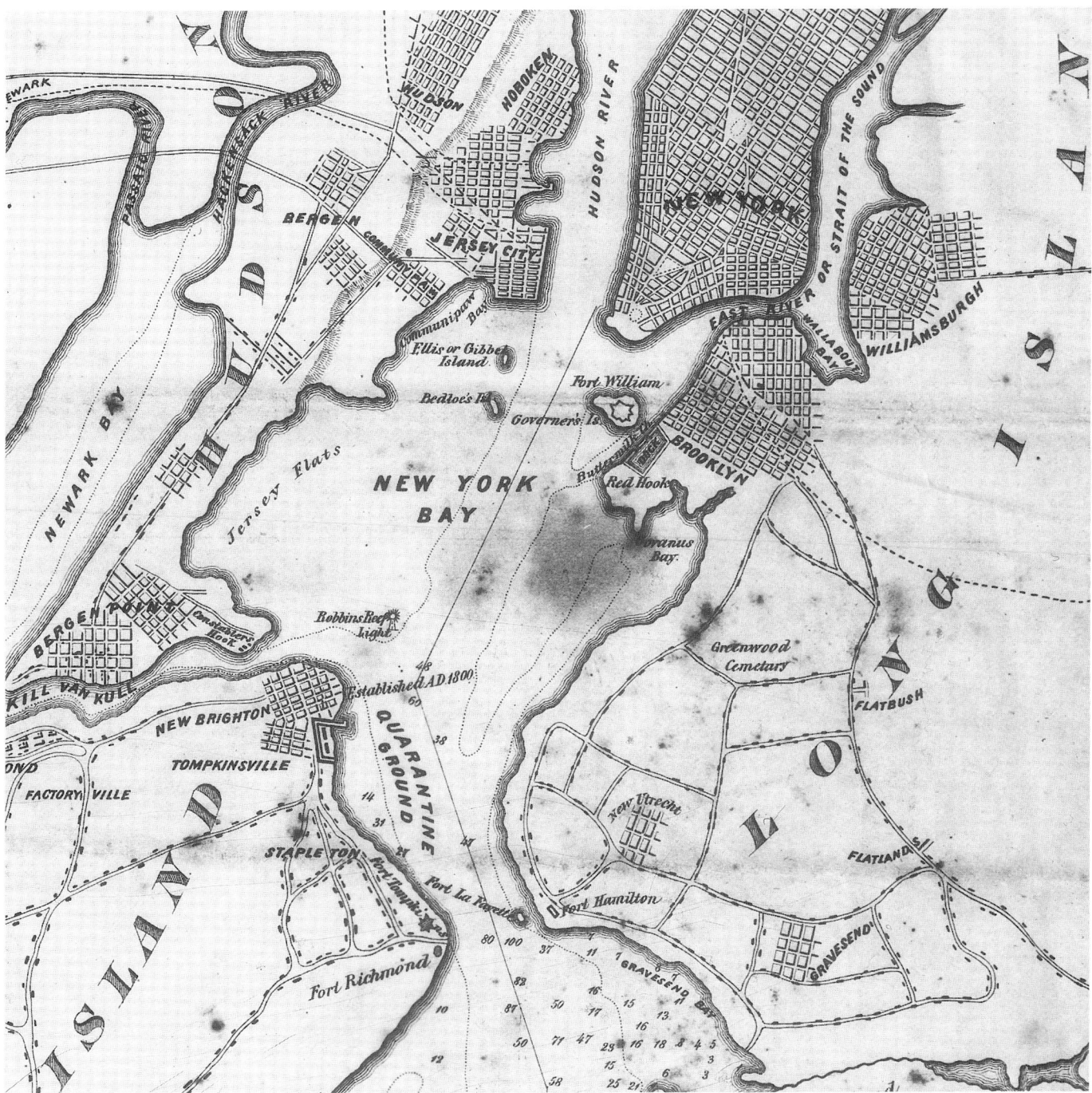

11. New York Bay, 1856
An 1856 map of New York Bay shows the choice location obtained by the Trustees when they purchased the Housman farm on Staten Island in May of 1831. Bordered by the Kill van Kull, the site offered excellent views of the busy shipping channel and New York harbor, and was easily accessible from Manhattan by ferry. The area soon became New Brighton, a suburb and summer resort.

12. Sailors' Snug Harbor, 1833

A woodcut print of Snug Harbor's first building was made shortly after it opened in 1833. The Greek Revival style building is the earliest known work by the New York architect Minard Lafever. On August 1, 1833, the newly completed Harbor received thirty-seven retired seamen, one of whom stands before the building and its ship mast flag pole. A reporter attending the opening ceremonies described the new building:

> This building, erected for the reception of 'aged and worn-out infirm seamen,' is the centre of the contemplated edifice; it is 65 feet by 100, three stories high including the basement, has a handsome marble front, with eight pillars or columns, containing thirty-four rooms, including those for washing and cooking; those intended for sleeping apartments are large and airy, furnished with everything necessary for convenience and comfort. The building is of the best materials, and the work done in the most faithful manner.

13. New Brighton, 1838

An 1838 panoramic view from the New York harbor and the Kill van Kull depicts the original 1833 Snug Harbor building and the elegant surrounding neighborhood of New Brighton. (Snug Harbor is the single building with flagpole, center right.) The village, with its Greek Revival mansions and the huge Pavilion Hotel (the three-part domed building, center left) was named by its developers after the English resort of Brighton. A European visitor remarked of New Brighton in 1837, "Seen from afar this little town appears magnificent; one would take it for a large city built by the Greeks or the Romans, so great is the number of its columns...." New Brighton's convenient location is cited as an advantage by the developers of the area in early advertisements, "Five miles from New York City traversed throughout the day by two swift and beautiful steamboats, the 'New Brighton' and the 'Water Witch,' in a period of twenty minutes." One of the boats is depicted here with steam and smoke billowing out of her stacks while unloading near the hotel.

14. Sailors' Snug Harbor, 1842
In this 1842 view of the Harbor the first building is flanked by the two wings that formed part of Lafever's original design. A granite obelisk in honor of Randall stands in front of the main building. Outside the iron fence a fashionably clad couple ride along the shore road.

15. Sailors' Snug Harbor, 1898
16. Sailors' Snug Harbor, 1907

By the turn of the century Sailors' Snug Harbor had vastly expanded, as indicated in a bird's-eye view of 1898 and map of 1907. It had become the "haughtiest and richest charitable institution in the world." Housing nearly a thousand men, it had grown enormously rich from the rental of Randall's Manhattan land. The residents considered themselves independently wealthy, inhabiting as they did this grand "resort" with dozens of buildings of every description amid beautifully landscaped grounds. Although several skilled architects were involved at various intervals, the complex arose without the benefit of a master plan.

The earliest main building with its two wings (C, B and D) was situated near the Kill van Kull within easy reach of the dock and shore road, and faced in a northeasterly direction toward the distant view of the New York harbor. These buildings served as the focus around which the later ones were constructed. In 1846 the Governor's and Physician's houses were built "on a line" with them but brought forward slightly toward the shore. (The Physician's House on the eastern side was demolished in 1885 and does not appear in the bird's-eye view.) In 1855 a large Dining Hall (G) was placed centrally behind the main building and the chapel erected in line with it to the east. (The chapel was later moved 200

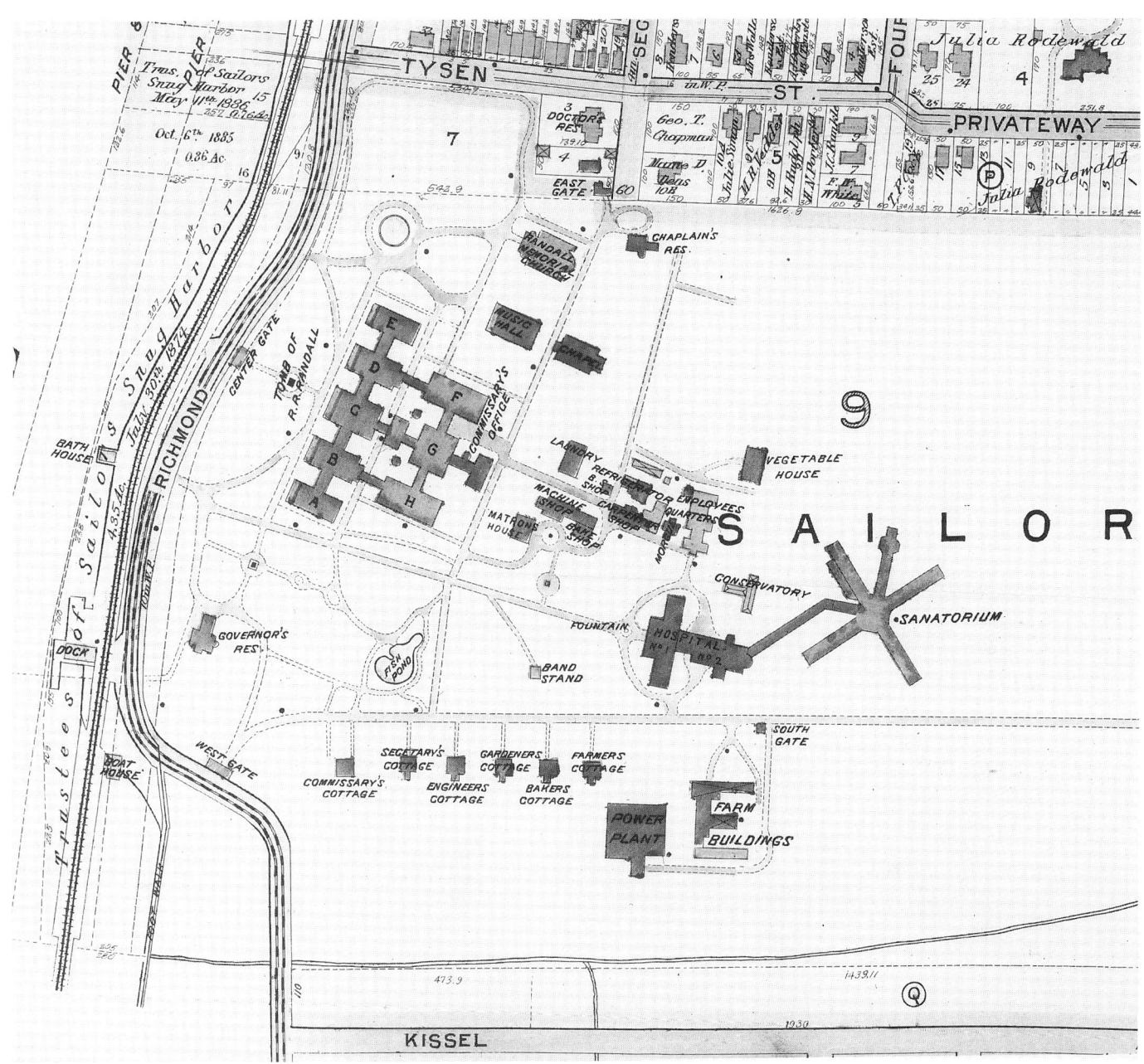

feet south, where it is shown here.) In 1876 and 1878 two large dormitories (F and H) were added on either side of the Dining Hall and in 1879 and 1880 two dormitories (A and E) with Greek Revival porticos were added on either side of the original three. The Church and Music Hall, completed in 1893, are aligned with the row of Greek Revival buildings, but set back to accommodate their large scale and to create a dramatic space for the eastern side of the property.

The Hospital begun in 1850, was located apart southwest of the main buildings, presumably for reasons of quiet and isolation. This building was enlarged with wings in 1879, and in 1885 an additional building was added behind it. In 1898 an enormous x-shaped sanitorium was begun at the rear of the hospital complex and joined to it by a long corridor.

The service buildings located behind the central complex—the laundry, matron's house, engine house, blacksmith shop and the morgue—appear informally arranged but in part aligned with the northeasterly direction of the main buildings. The farm buildings and power house on the west, the 1885 employees' cottages and the 1890 chief steward's house are aligned with the north-south lane.

47

17. Waterfront, c.1884
The side paddle steamboat the *Thomas W. Hunt* unloads at Snug Harbor's dock in this 1884 photograph. A boating house for pleasure craft built and used by neighboring citizens stands in the center, while Snug Harbor's dock house is partially hidden behind it. The North Shore Ferry Co.'s steamboats, which stopped three times a day at the dock, were the main access to the property until 1886. After that date the present-day St. George dock was developed for the Staten Island ferry and Snug Harbor was more often approached by railroad and street car.

18. Dock House, c.1910
The dock house, illustrated in a 1910 postcard, was built in 1879 and used as a waiting room for ferry passengers and as living quarters for the dock attendant.

19. Gatehouse, c.1910
Another 1910 postcard shows the main entrance to the Harbor, the gatehouse and fence. The seven-foot-high fence begun in 1842 eventually encircled twenty acres of the property. It is made of wrought and cast iron with granite footing and gateposts, and was designed by Frederick Diaper, an English architect who had recently immigrated to New York. Diaper patterned the fence after the Cumberland Gates at Hyde Park, London. The arch and lantern over the gateposts was a later addition to Diaper's design.

Built in 1874, the gatehouse served as a room for the gate attendant who checked each entrant. Its Italianate design with brackets beneath the eaves, quoins, barrel-vaulted walkway, cupola with ruby red glass, wrought-iron cresting and the French Empire-style dormers is an excellent example of vernacular Victorian architecture.

20. Sailors' Snug Harbor, c.1884

Harbor residents of the 1880s relax on the lawn between the gatehouse and the main dormitories. The beauty of the buildings does not occupy the men, as an 1882 account from *Harper's* indicates:

> A group of weather-beaten old sailors sat in the shade of a generous elm on the north shore of Staten Island, and placidly smoked their pipes in the heat of the mid-day sun. They were battered and maimed and aged, and showed the effects of tempestuous lives in wrinkled faces and knotted hands, but they smoked in the calm contentment of men who had no further cares, and were pleasantly drifting onward without anxiety.
>
> Before them was the Kill van Kull, alive with craft of every kind, from the monstrous excursion steamers, throbbing and thumping heavily toward Coney Island, to the slender racing shells that shot spasmodically about. Occasionally a cleanly built yacht would bowl up the channel, with the water hissing over her bows and bubbling wildly astern, or a staunch freight schooner or brig would sail majestically by the little group of aged seamen lounging under the shady elm. Then a short and stumpy old man, with a tanned face, a wooden leg and a single eye would struggle to his feet, whip a rickety spy-glass from his copious coat pocket, and bring it to bear gravely on the craft, though it might be less than fifty feet away. His companions always ceased talking when he did this, and looked up at him with grave and portentous interest. When he had finished sighting the craft, the one-eyed sailor would jam his glass together with a resounding smack, drop it into his pocket, and resume his seat with pursed lips and a puckered brow. His companions then looked at each other and slowly shook their heads, implying forcibly that the one-eyed sailor had his opinions, but he didn't shout them aloud and scatter them broadcast to the world. (*Harper's Weekly*, August 12, 1882, p.506.)

21. Sailors' Snug Harbor, 1920

A 1920 photograph reveals the continuity of life at Snug Harbor. Old sailors still congregate on the benches around the grounds and chat, much as they had decades earlier.

22. Sailors' Snug Harbor, c.1900

Edward Clegg, a resident of the Harbor between 1896 and 1901, took this group portrait in 1901. He also took individual portraits of each Harbor resident, but unfortunately none of these photographs has been located today. Clegg found life at Snug Harbor much to his liking and in a letter written to the Trustees in 1905 described them as "the best friends I have in the world."

23. Admission of an Old Sailor to the Harbor, 1873

To gain admission to the Harbor a seaman first submitted an application to the Trustees. If accepted, he came to the Governor's office to be enrolled. In this 1873 lithograph a new resident eager to sign the log book approaches Governor Melville with his application in hand, including proof of his having sailed on an American ship at least five years. Behind him others wait their turn for admission.

The first page of the log book provides the following information about those admitted when the institution opened in 1833:

> Samuel Newman, native of Falmouth, England, aged 61...
> Peter Nelson, New York, age 55, crippled by rheumatism;
> William Collins, from Prussia, age 60, same complaint,...
> George Thompson, Connecticut, 29, weak knees;...
> James Webster, England, 45, frost-bitten;
> George Whitley, Louisiana, 23, blind;
> John Smithers, 32, Maine, lost a leg;
> J. Chambers, Ireland, 64, lost an eye;
> John Freeman, France, 58, lame.

In addition to the ills usually associated with old age, younger men disabled from accidents at sea were also admitted. They were from all parts of the United States, and, as the list suggests, of many nationalities.

24. One of the Sleeping Rooms, 1873

Early residents slept in large dormitory-like rooms, as an 1873 scene illustrates. Ample space and light—and room for each man's possessions—created a home-like quality, a striking contrast for the retired sailor accustomed to crowded shipboard conditions.

That Snug Harbor provided a much-needed home for many a destitute or injured sailor is poignantly revealed in this sailor's account of his life following a disabling accident at sea:

> 'I went high an' I went low, lookin' fur a helpin' hand, but no one would give me a lift. My leg was shattered above the knee, an' I had to use two crutches, so of course I was no good at sea. I was left in Harve until my money an' credit was gone. Then I went over on the charity of an ol' shipmate to England, where I hoped to git relief from the firm which owned the *Percy B*, the ship I sailed as cap'n on fur six year. The firm gave me three pounds sterlin', an told me not to come back. Then I wandered about the docks lookin' fur my old friends. I didn't find them. No, it was no use; they couldn't be found. I hung around Liverpool fur two year, an' actually had to beg from door to door—me as once commanded a ship! Then I cum over to this side of the water, where I first started out to sea when a boy. I tell you it went hard with me fur a long time. I had no relations nearer than cousins, an' what cousin is goin' to take care of a

> middle-aged cripple old seamun? I peddled matches, an' hung around Water and South Streets fur years, gittin' lower all the time. Sometimes I'd meet some of the old men that sailed before the mast when I was cap'n of the *Percy B*, an' they'd give me a lift fur a time. Well, I got the rheumatism in my joints, an' it did appear to me as if there wasn't any use a-livin', when the owner of a sailors' boardinghouse in Cherry Street, who knew me, sez one day, 'Try the Snug 'Arbor,' sez he. I went down, an' they took me in because I was crippled, an' washed me an' shaved me, an' give me a room as clean as the cap'n's cabin of a man-o-war, an' put me inside of a new suit of clothes, stuck a pipe in my mouth, an' sez, 'There, you're safe an' sound forever, an' God bless your soul!' (*Harper's Weekly*, August 12, 1882)

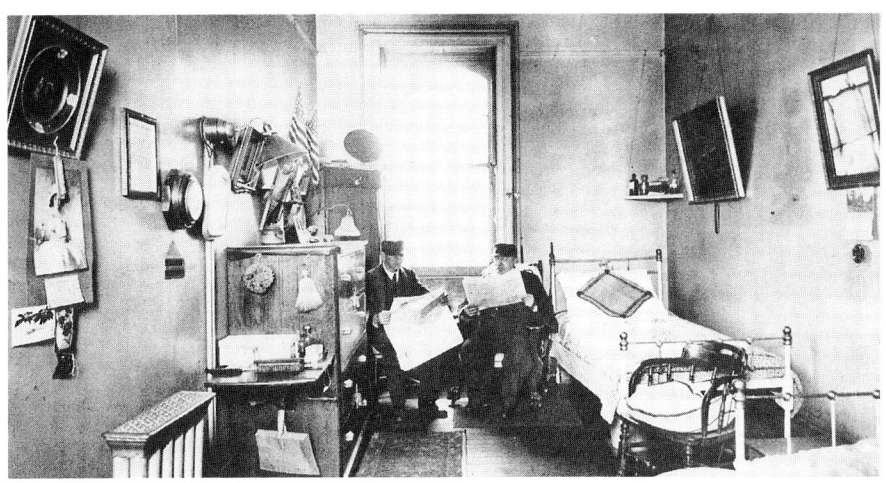

25. Bedroom, 1916
When new dormitories were built, residents enjoyed single or double rooms. Here in a photograph of 1916 two residents read newspapers beside their sunny window. Their well-kept room is filled with memorabilia and personal supplies. On the left wall an early electric light fixture shares space with flags, clocks, pictures and calendars. All roommates did not co-exist as peacefully as these, however. Some reportedly drew chalk lines down the middle of the room to end hostilities. Many rivalries existed, particularly between the sailors and the steamboat men. The following story was reported by Geoffrey Hellman in the May 21, 1934, *New Yorker*.

> A year ago, Captain Martin Svendrup, an old wooden boat man, awoke to find his roommate, Captain James Pigott, diddling with the radiator. Captain Pigott was feeling cold. He removed the radiator cap and steam hissed into the room. 'Steam!' shrieked Captain Svendrup, and, bouding out of bed, he wacked Pigott over the head with his cane, knocking him senseless. The judge in police court subsequently suspended sentence, Captain Svendrup having served eleven days in the Richmond County Jail while awaiting trial. An attempt was made by the Court to get the two mariners to shake hands. Captain Pigott was agreeable, but Captain Svendrup stomped off indignantly, saying he could never forgive Pigott for having sent him to jail for such a trifling thing.

26. Hallway Outside Dining Room, c.1910
11:55 AM. Waiting for Dinner." Residents waiting for admission to the dining hall are shown seated along the corridor connecting to the front dormitories. The stained glass window in the main building appears at the end of the corridor.

27. The Dining Room, 1916

"Dinner on this particular day," commented an 1874 visitor, "consisted of mutton-stew, which was served up in large tin tureens." It appears from this photograph taken forty years later that the stew is still being served from the same tureens! The early by-laws contained many provisions for maintaining order in the dining rooms—the home-like atmosphere of the dormitories is not evident at these tables seating thirty men. The farm provided vegetables and fresh milk in the early days, but as the Harbor grew in size it had to purchase much of the food from outside sources.

28. Workroom, 1873
29. Workroom, 1884

30. Workroom, 1882
31. Workroom, c.1900
In addition to the scheduled mealtimes and prayer services, the residents spent a portion of each day in the dormitory workrooms making baskets, hammocks, mats and ship models, as shown in these scenes dating between 1873-1900.

32. The Reading Room, 1837
33. The Library, 1937

A library was established at Snug Harbor in 1841, when the Trustees appropriated $400 for books to be purchased by the clergy Trustees. Included in their purchases were works of fiction, history and travel, but most were devotional literature. "Cornelius the Centurian," "Breckenridge on Papism," and Blunt's "Life of St. Paul" are typical of the original titles. Over the years' the library grew to encompass several thousand volumes. Adjacent to it was the reading room where daily newspapers were available. The recreation building completed in 1918 included a huge hall for the library, with provision for listening to the radio on private earphones.

34. The Chapel, 1876

The chapel was constructed by a New York builder, James Salmon, and opened in 1856. Originally it lacked a tower and had only a simple two-columned porch as shown in the 1876 lithograph. A plain entablature, cornice and pilasters at the corner of the building were in keeping with the Greek Revival style of Snug Harbor's other buildings. The round-headed windows and colored glass suggest an additional influence—the Italianate Revival style. Salmon wanted to construct a tower for the chapel, as a discussion in the 1855 *Minutes* makes clear, but the Trustees did not give their approval. Salmon was completing two other buildings on the property at the time (the huge dining hall and a new wash house), and the Trustees may have felt that economy demanded that the tower be eliminated.

The present-day three-stage tower with belfry shown in the line drawing and marked at the top stage by slender columns, was constructed in 1883 by Snug Harbor's Head Carpenter, Richard Smyth, who may have designed it himself or used the original plan.

35. Chapel Interior, 1975
36. The Chapel, 1886

37. The Randall Memorial Church, 1899
38. Church Interior, 1899

The elaborate white marble church completed in 1893 is a striking indication of Snug Harbor's wealth at the close of the nineteenth century. The building became a Staten Island landmark and was visible even from the distant Battery in Manhattan. It was designed by Robert W. Gibson, the architect of the Albany Cathedral and many of New York's public buildings. A Snug Harbor tradition described the church as a one-sixth scale replica of St. Paul's Cathedral in London. But despite its Renaissance-style dome and twin towers, it was not a copy of the London church. Theodore Dreiser, who visited the Harbor in 1904, described the marble interior of the church as a "soothing sactuary of many colors."

In addition to the Sunday services, which were no longer compulsory by now, the church was also used for bi-monthly concerts and organ recitals. Dreiser reported on the lack of enthusiasm for religious activities among the residents:

> When Sunday comes not one out of ten attends religious services, and on organ recital nights it is hard to muster a corporal's guard. 'Yeh can't interest me in such rum-te-tum-tum stuff as them organ fellers grind off,' was the indifferent comment of one and concerning religion another said: 'I haint had much time for preachin' for sixty-eight years come now the first of June next, and I 'spec' I'll manage to weather it out and get to port without worryin' much about it—the little time I have left. I ain't disrespectful, you understand—just kind of set.

39. The Randall Memorial Church and Music Hall, c.1900
40. Music Hall Interior, c.1930

A photograph taken by Edward Clegg in 1900 shows the church with the Neptune Fountain in the foreground and the Music Hall on the right. In the Music Hall, bi-monthly entertainments were held featuring vaudevillians such as the Georgia Minstrels, the Hotchkiss sisters, and the Lyrolean Warblers. Other musical programs featured the Boston Ladies Schubert Quartette, the Amphion Ladies Quartette, and the Berkeley Ladies Quartette. Joshua Slocum, the first man to sail alone around the world, spoke here shortly after completing his historic voyage in 1897. Silent motion pictures were shown beginning in 1911, and "sound-on-film" equipment was installed in the Music Hall in 1933. Twice-weekly showings of motion pictures, extremely popular with the residents, were held in the Hall until 1965.

41. Sanitorium Interior, c.1901
42. Sailors' Snug Harbor, with Hospital in Foreground, c.1930
43. Sanitorium, 1904

If a resident required extended medical care it was available to him in Snug Harbor's hospital or sanitorium. The photograph of the sanitorium interior was made when the building opened in 1901. The sanitorium, presumably for the treatment of TB or other chronic diseases, was constructed on an x-shape plan allowing maximum light and cross ventilation for each ward. An enormous dome marks the crossing of the four wings.

44. The Governor's House, c.1910

Snug Harbor Governors lived in this imposing residence. Governor Thomas Melville's clan gathered here for their holiday celebrations.

Its thirty rooms included two parlors, a billiard room and library and required a staff of eight. A twin to this house was built for the physician on the eastern edge of the property. A keen rivalry must have existed between the Governor and the resident physician, for each time improvements were made to one house (new wallpaper, or paint, adding a bay window, or a piazza or marble mantle), a similar change was ordered for the other house. The houses were designed by Willian Ranlett, a Staten Island architect, and built in 1846. However, later additions greatly changed the original appearance of the houses.

45. Road Leading to the Graveyard, 1979
46. Graveyard, 1979

Snug Harbor's cemetery is approached by a tree-lined road running to the back of the property. A long-time neighbor remembers the small processions which passed at regular intervals through the Harbor's south gate, on their way to the graveyard, with the dead man's casket accompanied only by the mortician, chaplain, or one or two friends. In the fall of the year many graves were dug at once in anticipation of winter's frozen ground. Today the road to the cemetery is interrupted by the suburb of Randall Manor, but hidden behind the well-kept houses the cemetery remains. The hillside sparsely dotted with grave markers is inadequate evidence of the thousands of men who are buried there. Gravestones recently damaged by vandals were removed and stored in the basement of the chapel.

This unsentimental attitude toward the dead reflects the reality confronted almost daily in an institution such as Sailors' Snug Harbor. By virtue of his vocation the sailor too has become familiar with death and may face it more openly than most men. A 77-year-old resident expressed the attitude in 1899: "We've met often enough, death and I, and I've always beaten him. I know that he must down me at last, and when that time comes—it can't be far off now—he'll find me waiting for him."

Phillip's 1856 sermon admonished the aged sailors to prepare for their heavenly voyage and Snug Harbor's chaplains continued his concern. Charles Jones, the chaplain between 1866 to 1895 kept an annual record of deaths in which he indicated the small percentage of those whom he considered ready for heaven. Even in these "roll calls," one of which follows, the chaplain's concern for statistical accuracy suggest a no-nonsense confrontation with death.

> To the Editor of the
> *Sailors' Magazine.*
> Dear Sir:
> I herewith transmit to you for publication the record of deaths among the inmates of the Sailors' Snug Harbor during the year 1891, as follows. The whole number is 105. As to their nationalities, 46 were born in the United States, 8 in England, 23 in Ireland, 7 in Scotland, 5 in Sweden, 4 in Germany, 2 each in Norway, Finland and St. Johns, N.F., and 1 each in France, Spain, Denmark, Manilla, Western Island, and Nassau, N.P.
>
> Of the whole number, 80 were Protestants, and 25 Catholics; 23 died in hopes of a better country, even a heavenly; of these 12 were hopefully converted after entering the institution and under my ministry.
>
> The sum of their ages was 6,981 years, giving an average of 66 years, 5 months and 2¾ days. The oldest was 96 and the youngest 40 at death. Three were over 90, 10 over 80, 38 over 70, 41 over 60, and under 50 only 2.

47. Air View, 1931

This aerial view of 1931 shows the Harbor little-changed from the bird's-eye view of 1898. The extensive vegetable gardens and farmlands can be seen. An interesting detail—the laundry drying on the line (the white grid)—appears in the center of the picture. The Snug Harbor entered the Great Depression with a surplus of $4 million, but after World War II changing patterns of health care for the aged, inflation and declining revenues from the Washington Square properties contributed to a decline in the Harbor's enrollment and its subsequent retrenchment.

48. Randall Memorial Church Demolition, 1952

Closed and in need of costly restoration, the Randall Memorial Church was demolished in 1952 after attempts to save it for community use were abandoned. The hospital, sanitorium, farm buildings and several service buildings had been demolished the previous year, and the Governor's Mansion was razed in 1955. In 1965 the Harbor's Trustees announced plans for a modernization of its facilities which would entail the demolition of many of the remaining buildings. Five of the Greek Revival buildings and the chapel received New York City Landmark designations which were sustained by the courts and demolition averted. In 1976 the Trustees announced plans to relocate in North Carolina, and the land and principal buildings were sold to the City of New York.

49. Front Buildings, Rear Elevation, c.1966

50. Front Buildings, 1973

51. Fence, 1973
52. Dome, Main Hall, 1975

53. Recreation Hall Interior, 1975

Bedroom, 1916

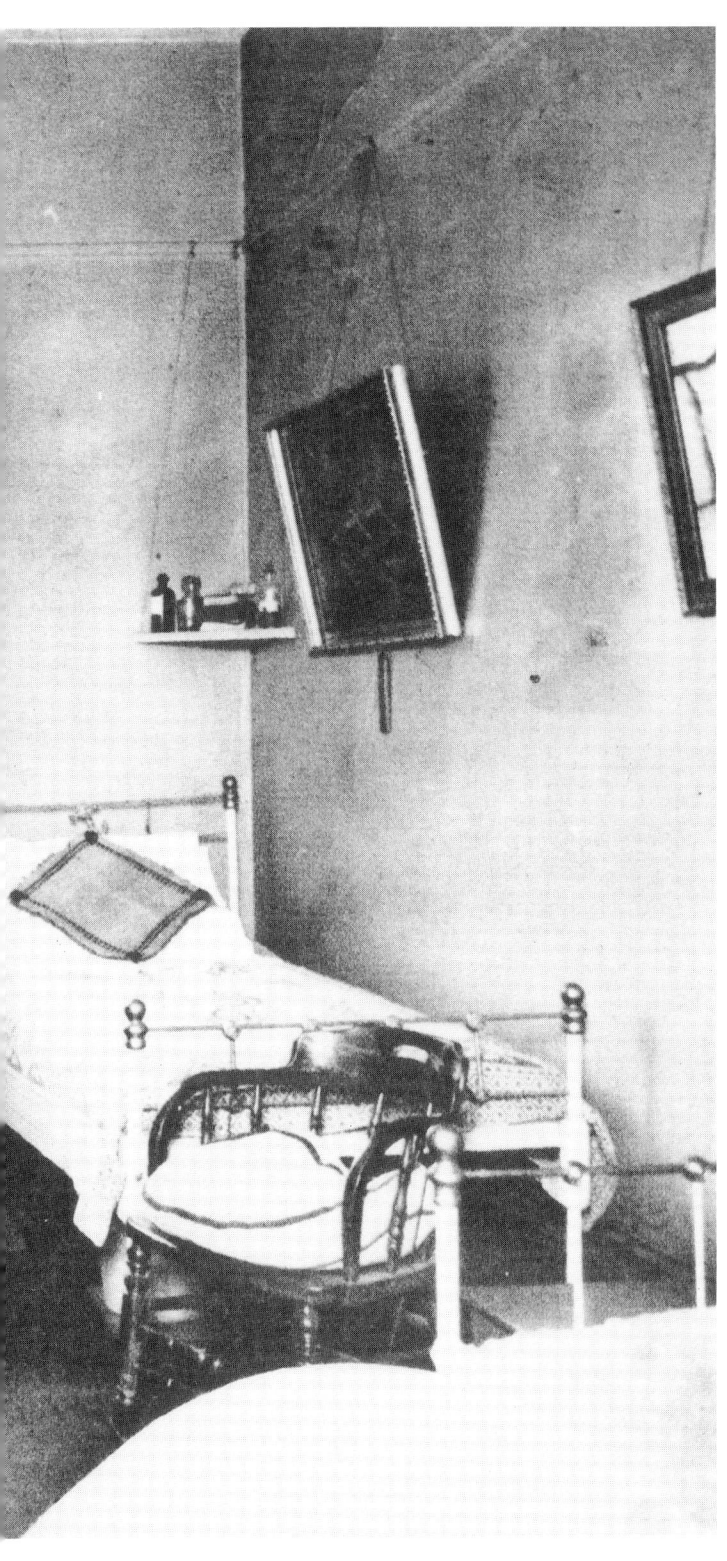

Part III
Snug Harbor
Anthology

Introduction

This anthology is intended as a contemporary record of life at Snug Harbor. It records conversations and impressions that cannot be reproduced by a modern writer. The published writings of two former Sailors' Snug Harbor residents convey, as no "land lubbers" can, the sailors' pride in the adventures and mishaps of his vocation.

Louis Bagger's article in *Harper's New Monthly Magazine* presents Snug Harbor on a winter day in 1872. During his ferry ride to Staten Island and later on a tour of Snug Harbor's buildings we are introduced to several residents and Captain Melville, who explains the practice of taboo.

Theodore Dreiser, one of America's most celebrated novelists, wrote three essays on Snug Harbor. The first of these borrowed heavily from an article written by Franklin North in 1884. Dreiser's second essay, printed in 1903 in the Sunday gravure section of the *New York Tribune,* gives a lighthearted account of the institution and its founding. The third, which is shortened slightly here, was included in *The Color of a Great City,* a collection of essays on New York City scenes.

In "When the Sails Are Furled" Dreiser presents a somber interpretation of the Harbor and its residents. He places little emphasis on the adventurous former life of the residents and their colorful vocabulary, but stresses primarily their discontent with old age. He describes them as independent and restless; some occasionally suffering from "pure cussedness," swearing loudly, drinking too much, and snoring in church. But it is primarily their restlessness in the face of old age and death that fascinates Dreiser. The beauty of the buildings and the orderliness of the institution only heightens Dreiser's awareness of the sailors' remorse over their loss of freedom.

Eight Bells, the title of Frank Water's book, is a nautical term referring to the end of the sailors' work shift, and beginning of the rest period. Waters, who was born around 1855 and was a resident of Snug Harbor in the 1920s, records familiar stories that were enjoyed by the seamen as they reminisced about their sailing days. In the story reproduced here Captain Knowles describes New York City waterfront life in the 1850s, and his experience of being "shanghaied" aboard the *Sultana.* A subplot involves a spree in Rangoon played out by one of Knowles' shipmates, Patty Mullins, and a rumdrinking elephant.

William Morris Barnes, who also lived at Snug Harbor in the 1920s writes in a conversational manner about his experiences as a windjammer sailor. In the first selections here he tells of a childhood voyage and presents his defense for the seagoing vocation.

In a later chapter he tells of his apprenticeship aboard the windjammer *Miranda* which began when he was fourteen. We learn how the captain teaches his new crew members the skills required by a sailor and how he endures the hardships of a long voyage. In the final pages of his book Morris speaks of the sailor's readiness for death.

THE SAILORS' SNUG HARBOR.

"THIS is rather a cold morning, isn't it?" "Cold, Sir? She's a *biter*. Bless me if my toes ain't a'most a-comin' off with cold!"

This was rather a curious remark, seeing that it came from a person whose lower extremities consisted of two wooden sticks from the knees down. I suppose that my countenance betrayed my astonishment at it, for the old sailor smiled, and, looking down at his sticks, continued:

"You see, Sir, somehow or other the cold weather always loosens my straps, and I feel as if the pins were goin' to shake me off. My old uns, of the real stuff, were left at San Juan d'Ulloa, in the Mexican war, and since then I have been hoppin' around on pedestals. But there's the Harbor now, Sir, and that's where I have been anchored these twenty years. Nice place, commodore. Was you ever there?"

I told the old man that it was just the object of my visit at the present time, and that I had come down on the boat for no other purpose. I also told him that I had a letter to Governor Melville, and that I should be obliged to him if he could show me where to find that gentleman.

Meanwhile the boat approached the landing, the gang-plank was drawn ashore, and heavy boxes, barrels, and bundles, containing provisions for the Harbor, were being carried on shore. Huge carcasses of beef and mutton came next, and after that came the living freight for the Harbor. My friend seized his crutches, and coming up close to me, whispered into my ear: "Say, commodore, you are goin' to call upon the gov'nor, ain't you? Now, Sir, I will tell you how you could do a service to an old salt, if you wanted to. There's Jack Stubbs; he rooms with me, and has got a wooden leg like me (but only one), and has been *tabooed* acause he came home half-seas-over the other night. It was his old man's birthday, you see, and he had been celebratin' it up in the city. Now, Sir, if you could lay in a good word for him with the gov'nor, saying that he didn't mean to do it, but that he was overtook suddenly, or somethin' of that sort, I think that the gov'nor would let 'im off cheap. Do what you can, commodore; Jack is a good boy, although he *does* love the bottle!"

I promised to do as asked, and we went together through the iron gate, and up the smooth walk leading to the centre or main building of the "Sailors' Snug Harbor." On our way thither I learned that the "boy," Jack Stubbs, for whose benefit I had promised to interfere, was eighty-two years old, and that "celebrating the birthday of the old man" was only a slang term for getting a little the worse for liquor, "which will," my friend with the wooden legs said, "occasionally happen to some of 'em."

Ascending the broad marble steps, we entered a large hall in the main building, lighted from above by a large oval window in the cupola, and occupied with chairs and benches placed across the floor, and leaving a narrow passage-way along the wall on either side. Just inside the door, and fronting the benches, was a reading-desk of oak with a red velvet cushion, and in the rear stood, on either side of the opposite door, two vases of terra cotta, filled with shrubs and flowers. A gallery went round the hall on all sides, at the height of the second floor, and above that was the cupola and sky-light. A large portrait of Captain John Whitten, who had once gone from Albany direct to China in a small sloop, and who subsequently was the first governor of the Harbor (from 1833 to 1844), faces the main entrance from the gallery; and above that is a well-executed bust, in marble, of the founder of this grand institution, Captain Robert Richard Randall.

"This way, Sir, to the gov'nor's office!" and my friend hobbled round to the right, and knocked at a door facing the hall; "and don't forget to lay in a word for Jack Stubbs, now, commodore, *if* you please," he had just time to repeat, in a whisper, when a loud "Come in!" summoned me to enter. It was a snug and comfortable office, seated in which, before a bright fire, was the genial governor of the Sailors' Snug Harbor, Captain Thomas Melville.

After the usual salutations, I delivered my letters and credentials, and had at once a cordial welcome extended to me. Feeling comfortable and at ease after my rough and cold trip down on the boat, I did not forget my promise to my fellow-passenger with the wooden legs, but related to the governor the promise that had been exacted from me. He laughed, and promised to forgive old Stubbs for this once, "although," he said, "he is one of the worst we have, on account of his intemperance, notwithstanding his age. By making baskets he earns enough to go on a regular spree every fortnight, and if we put no restrictions upon him, the probability is that he would 'celebrate the old man's birthday' some two dozen times a year. By 'tabooing' him is meant that he is not permitted, for a certain term, to go outside the iron railing. There is only about a week left of his term, and, as you desire it, I shall willingly forgive the old man that, and put him upon his good behavior."

It must be said, however, in justice to the inmates of the Harbor, that their conduct, with but very few exceptions, is irreproachable in every respect. It but seldom becomes necessary to *taboo* any body, and a still rarer occurrence is the expulsion of any. This last measure is only resorted to in cases where repeated drunkenness or disorderly and violent conduct renders it absolutely necessary. Out of a population in the Harbor of more than four hundred inmates, only five or six cases of expulsion occur in a year.

There were, at the time of my visit, 396 inmates in the Harbor, of all ages and belonging to all nationalities. Paragraph XI. of the by-laws of this institution declares: "All mariners, including captains and mates, if aged, decrepit, and worn-out sailors, are the proper objects of this trust. But no person shall be admitted as an inmate of the institution (if a foreigner born) who can not furnish satisfactory proof of his having sailed for at least five years under the flag of the United States;" and this further stipulation is made: "No person shall be received as a member of this institution who is a habitual drunkard, or whose character is immoral, or who labors under any contagious disease."

These are the only conditions regulating the admission of worn-out old mariners into the Sailors' Snug Harbor. By the charity and generosity of the founder, Captain Randall, the gates of this snug harbor are open to every nationality and every creed. Of the 396 inmates above mentioned, only 197 were native Americans, and these were of an average age of 57 years; the balance was mostly made up from the following nationalities:

England, 44, of an average age of 54 years.
Ireland, 33, " " " 48 "
Scotland, 14, " " " 53½ "
Germany, 24, " " " 55 "
Sweden, 26, " " " 57 "
Norway, 10, " " " 50½ "
Denmark, 10, " " " 53 "

Then there were some from Poland, Malta, Cape de Verd, and the Cape of Good Hope. The average age of the inmates is 55 years; the youngest man in the institution was a young sailor of about 23, who had lost his sight by an accident, and the oldest was a colored man named Jacob Morris, who, at the time of my visit, had attained the ripe old age of 103 years.

Every morning at seven o'clock a bell calls all the inmates down to breakfast, which consists of a quart of excellent coffee for each, and an abundant supply of home-made bread and butter. Dinner is on the table at twelve, and supper at half past five or six P.M., according to the season. At nine in the evening all the lights must be put out, except the lamps in the halls and in the hospital, and the inmates are expected to retire to rest. Except when *tabooed* or on the sick-list, every inmate is at liberty to leave the institution, and visit his friends in the city or elsewhere. All he is required to do is to report to the governor before leaving and upon his return. The gates are open for visitors every day during the week from nine in the morning till nine in the evening, except on Sundays, when no visitors are received.

The inmates were at their dinner in the large and attractive dining-hall when we entered it. This is situated on the ground-floor of a large building in the rear of the main or central building, with which it communicates by a wooden bridge, raised about ten feet above the ground. The largest dining-room contains twelve long tables, each of which can accommodate thirty-two diners. In another dining-room opposite there are four tables, each capable of accommodating the same number. The dinner on this particular day consisted of mutton-stew, which was served up in large tin tureens. The spoons and forks were of the best white metal, each bearing the stamp "Sailors' Snug Harbor," and the quality of the dinner was excellent. Each man had a tumbler of water in front of his plate, and of bread and meat as much as he desired. The table-linen was perfectly white and clean, and altogether the appearance of the dining-hall was more like that of a good substantial hotel than of a charitable institution.

Grace was said before dinner, and thanks were also offered after meals. Waiters, in long white aprons, were busily engaged among the tables in removing empty dishes and substituting filled and steaming ones in their places. Satisfaction and happiness shone in the face of every one; and I have no doubt that many an old sailor, at the bottom of his heart, on this cold and wintry day, silently blessed the memory of his benefactor.

There is nowhere another institution conceived in the same spirit of liberal and unlimited benevolence, the famous Greenwich Hospital not excepted; nowhere else does the old sailor, after having braved many a storm and frequently faced death, find so safe and snug a harbor. There, seated in a warm and comfortable room, he can through the window look out upon the scenes of his former life as a mariner; there is the deep blue sea, covered with numerous craft, reminding him of the time when he himself braved its dangers, and recalling adventures in foreign climes, that, sitting there by the window in his easy-chair, he is fond of relating.

The greater part of the ground-floor in the main building is occupied by the hall

THE SUNNY CORNER.

already described, which is used in the winter months for religious services every morning and night, thus obviating the necessity of heating the chapel except on Sundays. All the buildings are heated by hot air from furnaces in the basements. To the left of the hall is the reading-room, where all the leading dailies, weeklies, and magazines can be found; and behind that is the library, well stocked with books, mostly consisting of narratives of travel and adventure, and books of voyages and exploring expeditions. On the opposite side, to the right of the entrance, are the office and private room of the governor, and up stairs are the sleeping apartments, facing on the gallery. In the basement are long airy corridors and work-rooms, where a great part of the inmates are occupied in basket-making. This industry is carried on to a very great extent in this institution, as it is easy work, requiring no strength or special skill, and a pursuit in which the blind can also engage. The importance of this industry may be estimated from the fact that during a single year baskets were made by the inmates that sold in the market for very nearly $30,000, averaging an income of about $75 for each inmate. These baskets are bought up mostly by two large New York houses, and a considerable proportion of them, as also of the mats made there, are shipped to and sold in Boston. The materials used in the manufacture of mats and baskets (Spanish palm leaf and rattan) are bought by the inmates themselves, and the whole profit belongs to them individually, and is for the greater part spent for tobacco and in the purchase of minor comforts. One old salt from New Hampshire had acquired a private library, numbering some forty odd volumes, which he had in his room, nicely arranged in a bookcase of his own manufacture, with glass doors. His latest acquisition was the "History of Julius Cæsar," by the ex-Emperor Napoleon, bound in green and gold.

In the basement are also some of the wash-rooms, furnished with iron basins and large towels on rollers, where the old sailors perform their daily ablutions and make their toilet, as washing in the rooms is prohibited. Passing through the wide and airy corridors, we found about sixty old men, some of them blind, engaged in basket-making, while at one end of the hall sat a blind man preparing the palm leaf for use, by splitting it and drawing it between two sharp knives fastened into a block of wood before him, by which it is cut into a uniform thickness and width. At the foot of the stairs sat a man, apparently not very old, and in good health, busily engaged in finishing the centre piece of a knife-basket.

"Hallo, Davy!" Governor Melville hailed him, "how are baskets to-day?"

Davy, turning his lustreless eyes upon us, answered,

"Dull, gov'nor—a'mighty dull; haven't sold a basket this fortnight. Think I will leave the basket business and go into mats."

This man, whose name was David James, was, I learned, the oldest inmate in the institution (though not by any means the oldest man), he being one of the thirty original inmates. He was then twenty-seven years old, and has been an inmate of the Harbor for thirty-seven years.

Here we also found, engaged in basket-making like the rest, a veteran from the war of 1812, named Daniel Collins, who had been twice captured in American merchantmen by the English cruisers. Nearly opposite him, with a large mat upon his knees, with which he was busily engaged, sat Cornelius Rose, an old white-haired and white-bearded sailor, who joined the American navy in 1812, belonged to the schooner *Enterprise* when she was captured by the English brig *Boxer*, and was one of the crew of the frigate *President* when, under the command of Decatur, that gallant ship fought three English frigates. He belonged to the old *Constitution* for nine years, and took an active part in the Mexican and Florida wars. His records and papers show that he has participated in no less than *twenty-seven* conflicts.

Besides basket-making the old sailors have other means of making money, one of the most common of which is fishing. A large proportion of the money which they accumulate, as we have already said, goes for tobacco. Of course no sailor can be *tabooed* for smoking.

On our way up stairs again the governor pointed out to me the "Swedish lawyer," so called from his nationality, and the fact of his being, or considering himself as being, the bright particular star, concentrating within himself the erudition of the whole community. He seemed to be not unlike our friend Jack Bunsby, and at the very time when we passed him he was engaged in laying down his opinion to another sailor, and I seemed to hear the familiar words, "Whereby—if so—why not? The bearings of the observation lies in the application of it—awast, then!"

Crossing the bridge, we again enter the rear building, the basement of which is occupied by the kitchen, the store-room, steward's office, colored men's mess, and blind men's mess. Here, also, are the apartments in which the assistants and employés of the institution take their meals. The blind men have two waiters to attend to their wants and assist them; but beyond some help at table, they require no aid, but navigate the whole building, up stairs and down stairs, assisted only by a cane, with which they feel their way. Here we meet one of the most interesting of the blind men just coming from his dinner. It is Captain John M'Ewen, who in 1813, while belonging to the privateer *Vengeance* of New York, assisted at the capture of twenty-one British vessels. Afterward he became the captain of an East Indiaman, and was for many years a prominent, successful, and well-known master of ships in the East India trade. But misfortunes overtook him; he lost his sight, and consequently became unable to follow his profession, and he is now a much-esteemed inmate of the Harbor. Passing from this building, we cross the grounds to the hospital, stopping on the way to have a look at the steam-laundry and bakery.

The hospital is a magnificent and solid building of gray sandstone, built in the same style as the main building, with massive pillars supporting a portico over the entrance. In the basement are the kitchen and work-rooms for the convalescent patients who desire to work at their usual occupation—basket-making. On the first floor is a large hall with a gallery or promenade overhead, and also the mess-rooms; and the upper story is occupied by the wards, which are all large, light, and airy, and have five or six iron bedsteads in each. On entering we were met at once by old Webster, who is now in the ninety-fourth year of his age. He was admitted an inmate of the Sailors' Snug Harbor in 1844, then sixty-seven years old. It must be confessed that age has—as he said himself—"rather brought him

down." His mouth is toothless, his eyes watery and dim; but his white hair and long white beard give him a venerable appearance. He speaks with difficulty, and is perfectly helpless at table.

"Well, Webster, how goes it?" the governor said, approaching him and wiping off his beard, full of crumbs of bread from his dinner, with his pocket-handkerchief.

"A-a-all ri-ght, gov'-nor; b-but why don't the d-doctor c-come to see m-me?"

"Why, Webster, are you sick? If so, the doctor shall, of course, come to see you, and I will send for him at once."

"N-no, gov'-nor, I a-ain't sick; but I'm a-getting old!"

"Well, the doctor can't help that, you know; but if you feel sick or need the doctor's assistance, why, then, of course, you shall have it at once."

"No, gov'-nor, I d-don't want the d-doctor, if you will let me g-go out alone; I c-can t-tr-travel without a p-pilot!"

To this, however, the governor would not assent, much to the mortification of old Webster, who insisted that he was well enough to travel over to New York and come back again without an escort. He is at liberty to go out whenever he pleases if the weather is fair and nothing particularly is the matter with him; but he has always an assistant or a reliable brother inmate to accompany him and take care of him. This old man is, however, notwithstanding his age, of a very belligerent disposition; thus, a short time ago it became necessary to *taboo* him for a month because he knocked one of the patients on the head with his cane, getting excited during an argument over some small matter; and it was but a week previous to my visit that he challenged one of the younger boys of seventy-five outside to a personal combat as a means of settling a little difficulty between them.

We found lying in bed, in one of the wards, with a bowl of chicken soup on a small table beside him, an invalid, Charles Risby, Norwegian by birth, and seventy-seven years old. He arrived in this country at Boston on the day that the long embargo went into operation. During the war of 1812 he belonged to the *Constitution*, on board of which he participated in the fight with the *Guerrière*. In the same ward was Ebenezer Lakemann, who, while serving in the American privateer *Buckskin*, of Salem, Massachusetts, in 1813, captured the English schooner *Marianne*, which was recaptured, with him on board as prize-master, by the English frigate *Maidstone*. He was taken to England and imprisoned there, and afterward exchanged for one of the crew of the *Guerrière*.

In a ward on the opposite side of the hall, looking bright and cheerful, and ornamented with several bird-cages containing chirping and twirling canaries, we found old Jacob Morris (colored), who entered the Sailors' Snug Harbor in the year 1848, then at the age of eighty. He was now in the 104th year of his age, and had, until very lately, been well and up every day, walking around the grounds as one of the youngest. "But, gov'nor," he said, "me getting feeble, sah; bery feeble! Me can not now leave bed, sah; bery weak in de joints, sah; and bosom pangs here—*here!*" and he pressed his hands against the left side of his breast. It was evident that he could not live long.

The wards for the sick were all well lighted by windows reaching from the ceiling to the floor, and well heated and ventilated. Nearly every room had bird-cages and flowers in it, and the walls were painted a delicate lavender, pleasant to the eye, and imparting a soft and cheerful appearance to the room.

Leaving the hospital we proceeded to visit the farm belonging to this institution, and were accompanied thither by another old veteran, John Strain.

The products of the farm in 1870 amounted to $9067 60. Allowing for expenses for conducting and stocking it—$3768 87—there remained a net profit of $5298 73, which is a very handsome exhibit. Among the articles raised may be named 5465 eggs, 20,662 quarts of milk, 1722 bushels of potatoes, 5627 heads of cabbage, 2990 heads of lettuce, 16,410 cucumbers, besides great quantities of carrots, radishes, beets, corn, string-beans, onions, sweet-potatoes, squashes, water-melons, etc., etc. The live stock consisted of 12 milch cows, 4 young heifers, 1 Albany bull, and 90 hogs, besides oxen and horses. Of poultry there are kept about 70 chickens, mostly for the use of the hospital. An ice-house is also erected here, in which is stored away the ice for the use of the Harbor, which is obtained from a pond situated on their property.

Away back, south of these buildings, lies a fine stone building, belonging to a society of ladies in New York and on Staten Island, but erected upon ground belonging to the Sailors' Snug Harbor, which is occupied as a "Home for Destitute Seamen's Children." These ladies work in silence; there is no ostentation about the distribution of their charities. But they labor earnestly, and in a good cause.

The chaplain belonging to the Sailors' Snug Harbor lives with his family in a large and comfortable house situated on the premises, in the rear of the chapel, which was erected in 1855. Here services are held every Sunday during the winter, and every day, morning and night, during summer. The chapel is a plain but handsome brick building, without any cupola or belfry, but with large stained windows. The interior is plain, but scrupulously neat and tastefully decorated; and upon two long tablets, one on each side of the altar, are inscribed the names of all the trustees and officers that have been connected with the Harbor since its first opening.

The doctor also lives upon the premises, in a fine house situated near the road and facing the Kills, far in advance and to the right of the main buildings. The governor's house occupies a similar position on the opposite side, to the left of the main buildings; and from both of these dwellings a flagged walk leads to the main entrance of the centre building. Directly in front of this, surrounded by an iron railing, is the plain marble monument that covers the remains of the founder of this noble charity.

The old sailors are not allowed to keep dogs. To some of them this is a great deprivation. These lovers of the canine species are obliged to gratify their peculiar tastes outside the limits of the institution. With one of them, known as "the bone man," the passion for dogs amounts to a monomania. In order to render himself attractive to his favorites he fills his pockets with bones and wanders off into obscure haunts and by-ways, where he may often be seen surrounded and followed by his not entirely disinterested clients.

That the revenues of the Sailors' Snug Harbor in the course of time will be largely increased when the long leases shall have expired, and their up-town property be released on more favorable terms than at present, there can be no doubt; and this will, of course, admit of a still further extension of the institution, and the accommodation of a still greater number of aged, decrepit, and worn-out sailors. The greater part of Mr. Stewart's store, situated on Broadway and Tenth Street, in New York, is erected upon leased ground owned by the Sailors' Snug Harbor, as are also many other costly stores and buildings in the upper part of the city. The resources of the institution are very ample, and they are honestly and judiciously applied in accordance with the design of the testator, being in the hands of gentlemen well known for their integrity, and of the highest social standing.

As I left I was accompanied to the gate by an old veteran, who told me that his name was John Perz, and that he had been captured and taken to England as a prisoner in 1814 by the British ship of the line *Elizabeth*, of seventy-four guns; and just as I got outside the gate somebody seized my hand and said, "Thank you, Sir, thank you; much obliged, Sir!" and turning round I beheld my friend of the morning on his two stumps, in company with the delinquent Jack Stubbs, who held his hat in his hand, looking somewhat sheep-faced, and staring at the knob at the end of his wooden leg. The governor had kept his promise: he was outside the iron railing, and consequently no longer *tabooed*.

THE COLOR OF A GREAT CITY

THEODORE DREISER

Illustrations by
C. B. FALLS

BONI AND LIVERIGHT
PUBLISHERS :: :: NEW YORK

WHEN THE SAILS ARE FURLED

The waters of the open sea as they rush past Sandy Hook strike upon the northeasterly shore of Staten Island, a low-lying beach overshadowed by abruptly terminating cliffs. Northeastward, separated by this channel known as The Narrows, lies Long Island. As the waters flow onward, following the trend of the shoreline of Staten Island, they become less and less exposed to the winds of the sea, and soon, as they pass the northernmost end of the island, they make a sharp bend to the west, passing between it and Liberty Statue, where the tranquil Kill von Kull separates the island from New Jersey.

Long ere they reach this region the sea winds have spent their force, and the billows, which in clear weather are still visible far out, have sunk to ripples so diminutive that the water is not even disturbed. And here, in Staten Island, facing the Kill von Kull, still stands in almost rural quiet and beauty Sailors' Snug Harbor. Long ago this was truly a harbor, snug and undisturbed, a place where the storm-harried mariner, escaping the moods and dangers of the seven seas, found a still and safe retreat. To-day they come here, weary from a long life voyage, to find a quiet home. And truly it is restful in its arrangements. The grounds are kempt and green, the buildings pleasingly solemn, and the view altogether lovely, a mixture of land and sea.

In the early days this pleasantly quiet harbor was a long distance from New York proper. Staten Island was but thinly settled, and the Kill von Kull a passageway seldom used. To-day craft speed in endless procession like glorious birds over the great expanse of water. On a clear day the long narrow skyline of New York is visible, and when fogs make the way of the pilot uncertain the harbor resounds with endless monotony of foghorns, of vessels feeling an indefinite way.

Though the surroundings are pastoral, the appearance of the inmates of this retreat, as well as their conversation, is of the sea, salty. Housed though they are for the remainder of their days on land, they are still sailors, vain of their service upon the great waters of the world and but little tolerant of landlubbers in general. To the passer-by without the walls they are visible lounging under the trees, their loose-fitting blue suits fluttering light with every breeze and their slouch hats pulled rakishly over their eyes, an abandon characteristic of men whose lives have been spent more or less in direct contact with wind and rain. You may see them in fair weather pacing about the paths of the grounds, or standing in groups under the trees. Upon a long bench, immediately in front of the buildings, others are sitting side by side, smoking and chatting. Many were captains, not a few common sailors. But all are now so aged that they can scarcely totter about, and hair of white is more often seen than that of any other shade.

For a period of nearly a year—a spring, summer and fall—I lived in the immediate vicinity of this retreat and was always interested by the types of men finally islanded here. They came, so I was told, from nearly all lands, France, Germany, Sweden, Norway, Finland, Iceland, Spain, Austria, Russia, and elsewhere, though the majority chanced to be of English and American extraction. Also, I was told and can well believe they are, a restless if not exactly a troublesome lot, and take their final exile from the sea, due to increasing years and in most instances poverty, with no very great equanimity. Yet the surroundings and the provision made for them by the founder of this institution, who, though not a sea-faring man himself, acquired his fortune through the sea over a century ago, are charming and ample; but the curse, or at least the burden of age and the ending of their vigor and activities, rests heavily upon them, I am sure. I have watched them about the very few saloons of the region as well as the coffee-houses, the small lunch counters and the moving picture theaters, and have noted a kind of preferred solitude and spiritual irritability which spells all too plainly intense dissatisfaction at times with their state. Among the quondam rovers are rovers still, men who pine to be out and away and who chafe at old age and the few necessary restraints put upon them. They would rather travel, would rather have the money it costs to maintain them annually as a pension, outside, than be in the institution. Not many but feel a sort of weariness with days and with each other, and I am quite convinced that they would be happier if pensioned modestly and set free. Yet this is a great institution and indeed a splendid benefaction, but it insists upon what is the bane and destruction of heart and mind: conformity to routine, a monotonous system which wears as the drifting of water and eats as a worm at the heart.

And yet I doubt if a better conducted institution than this could be found, or one more suited to the needs and crotchets of so many men. They have ample liberty, excellent food, clothing and shelter, charming scenery, and all the leisure there is. They are not called upon to do any labor of any kind other than that of looking after their rooms and clothes. The grounds are so ample and the buildings so large that the attention of every one is instantly taken. As you enter at the north, where is the main entrance, there is a monument to Robert Richard Randall, the founder of the institution. This marks his final resting-place; the remains of the philanthropist were brought here from St. Mark's Church in New York, where they had lain since 1825.

In the beginning there were but three buildings, which are to-day the central ones in a main group of nine. In toto, however, there are over sixty, situated in a park.

In a line, in the center of an eighteen hundred-foot lawn, stand the five main buildings, truly substantial and artistic. The view to the right and left is superb, tall trees shading walks and dividing stretches of lawn, with rows of benches scattered here and there. A statue by St. Gaudens beautifies the grounds between the main building and the governor's residence, while in another direction a fountain fills to the brim a flower-lined marble basin. Everywhere about the grounds and buildings are seen nautical signs and many interesting reminders of the man who willed the refuge.

The first little chapel that was built has long since been succeeded by an imposing edifice, rich in marbles and windows of stained glass. A music hall of stately dimensions, seating over a thousand people, graces a once vacant lawn. A hospital with beds for three hundred is but another addition, and still others are residences for the governor of the institution, the chaplain, physician, engineer, matron, steward, farmer, baker, and the buildings for each branch of labor required in the management of what is now a small city. In short, it has risen to the dignity of an immense institution, where a thousand old sailors are quietly anchored for the remainder of their days.

Some idea of the lavishness of the architecture can be had by entering the comparatively new church, where marble and stained glass are harmoniously combined. The outer walls are pure white marble, the interior a soothing sanctuary of many colors. Underfoot is a rich brown marble from the shores of Lake Champlain. The wainscoting is of green rep and red Numidian marble. Eight immense pillars supporting the dome are in two shades of yellow Etrurian marble, delicate and unmarked. The altar is of the same shade, but exquisitely veined with a darker coloring. Both chancel and choir floors are richly mosaiced, the chancel steps being of the same delightful coloring as the piers. To the left of the chancel is the pulpit, an octagonal structure of Alps green, with bands and cornices of Etrurian and Sienna marble supported on eight columns of alternate Alps green and red Numidian, finished with a brass railing and Etrurian marble steps. The magnificent organ, with its two thousand three hundred or more pipes, is entirely worthy its charming setting. Over all falls the rich, warm-tinted light from numerous memorial windows, each a gem in design and coloring. On one of these the worshiper is admonished to "Be of good cheer, for there shall be no loss of life among ye, but only of the ship."

Admonish as one may, however, the majority of the old seamen are but little moved by such graven beauty; being hardened in simple, unorthodox ways. Not a few of them are given to swearing loudly, drinking frequently, snoring heavily on Sundays and otherwise disporting themselves in droll and unsanctified ways. To many of them this institution appears to be even a wasteful affair, intended more to irritate than to aid them. Not a few of them, as you may guess, resent routine, duty, and the very necessary officials, and each other. Although they possess comfortable and even superior living apartments, wholesome and abundant food, good clothing, abundant clean linen, a library of eight thousand volumes, newspapers, periodicals, time and opportunity for the pursuit of any fad or fancy, and no restrictions at which a reasonable man could demur, still they are not entirely happy. Life itself is passing, and that is the great sorrow.

And so occasionally there is to be found in that portion of the basement room from which the light is debarred, looking out from behind an iron door upon a company of blind mariners who occupy this section, working and telling stories, a mariner or two in jail. And if you venture to inquire, his mates will volunteer the information that he is neither ill nor demented but troubled with that complaint which is common to landsmen and sailors, "pure cussedness." In some the symptom of this, I am told, will take the form of an unconquerable desire to go from room to room in the early morning and pull aged and irate mariners from their comfortable beds. In others it has broken out as a spell of silence, no word for any one, old or young, official or fellow resident. In another drunkenness is the refuge, a protracted spell, resulting in dismissal, with an occasional reinstatement. Another will fight with his roommate or his neighbor, sometimes drawing a chalk line between the two halves of a double room and defying the other to cross it at peril of his life. There have been many public quarrels and fights. Yet, all things considered, and age and temperament being taken into consideration, they do well enough. And not a few have sufficient acumen and industry to enter upon profitable employments. For there are many visitors, to whom useful or ornamental things can be sold. And a few of these salts will even buy from or trade with each other.

In consequence one meets with an odd type of merchant here and there. There is one old seaman, for instance, a relic of Federal service in " '61," whose chamber is ornamented to the degree of confusion with things nautical, most of which are for sale. To enter upon him one must pass through a whole fleet of small

craft, barks, brigs, schooners and sloops—the result of his jacknife leisure—arranged upon chests of drawers. Still another, at the time I visited the place, delighted in painting marine views on shells, and a third was fair at photography, having acquired his skill after arriving at the Harbor. He photographed and sold pictures of other inmates and some local scenes. Many can and do weave rugs and mats, others cane chairs or hammocks or fish-nets. Still others have a turn for executing small ornaments which they produce in great numbers and sell for their own profit. No one is compelled to work, and the result is that nearly all desire to. The perversity of human nature expresses itself there. In the long, light basement corridors, where it is warm and cozy, there are to be found hundreds of old sailors, all hard at work defying monotony with rapid and skilful finger movements.

All of these are not friendly, however, and many are vastly argumentative. No subject is too small nor any too large for their discussion in this sunlit forum. Especially are they inclined to belittle each other's experiences when comparing them with their own important past, and so many a word is passed in wrath.

"I hain't a-goin' to hear sich rubbish," remarked one seaman, who had taken offense at another's detailed account of his terrible experience in some sea fight of the Civil War. "Sich things ain't a-happenin' to common seamen."

"Yuh don't need to, yuh know," sarcastically replied the other. "This here's a free country, I guess, 'cept for criminals,—and they hain't all locked up, as they should be."

"So I thought when I first seed yuh," came the sneering reply, and then followed a hoarse chuckle which was only silenced by the stamping away of an irate salt with cheeks puffed out in rage.

Nearly all are irritatingly independent, resenting the least suggestion of superiority with stubborn sarcasm or indifference. Thus one, who owned his own ship once and had carefully refrained from whistling in deference to the superstitious line: "If you whistle aloud you'll call up a blow; if noisy you'll bring on a calm,'" met another strolling about the grounds exuberantly indulging a long-restrained propensity to "pipe the merry lay."

"I'll bet you wouldn't whistle aboard my ship," said he insinuatingly.

"Yeh! But I ain't aboard yer ship, thankee—I'm on my own deck." And "Haul in the bow lines; Jenny, you're my darling!" triumphantly swelled out on the evening breeze.

Down on the unplaned planks of the Snug Harbor wharf a score of old salts, regardless of slivers, sit the livelong day and watch the white-winged craft passing up and down. Being "square-riggers"—that is, having served all their lives aboard ship, barks and brigs—they look with silent contempt upon the fore and aft vessels of the harbor as they sail by. Presently comes, "Hello, Jim! Goin' to launch her?" from one who is contemplating with a quizzical eye a little weazened old man who comes clambering down the side of the dock with a miniature ship under his arm and a broad smile of satisfaction on his face.

"Ay, that's it," answers the newcomer. He has spent many weeks in building the little ship and now will be decided whether or not his skill has been wasted on a bad model. At once the critical faculty of the tars on the dock is engaged, and he of the boat becomes the subject of a brisk discussion. Sapient admonitions, along with long squirts of tobacco juice, are vouchsafed, the latter most accurately aimed at some neighboring target. Sarcasm is not wanting, the ability of the builder as well as the merit of his craft coming in for comment. The launching of such a craft has even engendered bitter hatreds and not a few fights.

We will say, however, that the craft is successfully launched and with sails full spread runs proudly before a light wind. In such a case invariably all the old sailors will look on with a keen squint and a certain tremor of satisfaction at seeing her behave so gallantly. Such being the case, the builder is at liberty to make a few sententious remarks anent the art of shipbuilding—not otherwise. And he may then retire after a time, proud in his knowledge and his very certain triumph over those who would have scoffed had they had the slightest opportunity.

I troubled to ask a number of these worthies from time to time whether, assuming they were young again, they would choose a sea-faring life. "Indeed I would, my boy," one answered me one morning. And another: "Not I. If I were to sail four thousand times I'd be as seasick the last trip as on the first day out. Every blessed trip I made for the first five years I nearly died of seasickness."

"Why did you keep it up, then?" I asked.

"Well, when I'd get into port everybody would ask: 'Well, how did you like it? Are you going again?' 'Of course I am,' I would answer, and went from pure shamefacedness and not to be outdone. After a while I didn't mind it so much, and finally kept to it 'cause I couldn't do anything else."

One of the old basket makers at the Harbor had occupied a rolling chair in the hospital and made baskets for nearly thirty-nine years. There was still another, ninety-three years of age, who would have been there forty years the summer I was there. And withal he was a most ingenious basket maker. One of the old salts kept an eating-stand where appetizing lunches were served, and he bore the distinction of having rounded the Horn forty-nine times in a sailing vessel. He was one of the few who possessed his soul in patience, resting content with his lot and turning to fate a gentle and smiling face.

"Will you tell me of an adventure at sea?" I once asked him.

"I could," he answered, "but I would rather tell you of thirteen peaceful years here. I came here when I was seventy, though at sixty, when I was weathering a terrible storm around the Cape with little hope of ever seeing the rising sun, I promised myself that if ever I reached home again I would stay there. But I didn't know myself even then. My destiny was to remain on the sea for ten years more, with this Harbor for my few remaining years. At that, if I were young I would go to sea again, I believe. It's the only life for me."

Back of all this company of a thousand or more, playing their last parts upon this little Harbor stage, is an interesting mechanism, the system with which the institution is run. There is a clothing department, where the sailors get their new outfits twice a year. I warrant that the quizzical old salt who keeps it knows every rent and tear in every garment of the Harbor. There is a laundry and sewing department, of which the matron has charge. There is a great kitchen, absolutely clean, where is space enough to set up a score of little kitchens. At four p.m. there are visible only two dignitaries in this savory realm. At that time one slices tomatoes and the other "puts on tea" for a thousand, the number who regularly dine here. The labor of cutting great stacks of bread is done by a machine. Broiling steaks or frying fish for a thousand creates neither excitement nor hurry. The entire kitchen staff numbers thirty all told, and the thousand sailors are served with less noise and confusion than an ordinary housewife makes in cooking for a small family.

There are separate buildings devoted to baking, vegetable storing and so forth, and the steward, farmer, baker and engineer, that important quartette, has each his private residence upon the grounds. The hospital, too, is a well-kept building, carefully arranged and bright and cleanly as such institutions can be made.

Passing this place, I have often thought what a really interesting and unique and beautiful charity it is, the orderly and palatial buildings, the beautiful lawns and flowers, and then the thousand and one characters who after so many earthly vicissitudes have found their way here and who, if left to their own devices, would certainly find the world outside a stormy and desperate affair. So old and so crotchety, most of them are. Where would they go? Who would endure them? Wherewith would they be clothed and fed? And again, after having sailed so many seas and seen so much and been so independent and done heaven only knows what, how odd to find them here, berthed into so peaceful a realm and making out after any fashion at all. How quaint, how naïve and unbelievable, almost. The blue waters of the bay before them, the smooth even lawn in which the great buildings rest, the flowers, the calm, the order, the security. And yet I know, too, that to the hearts of all of these, as to the hearts of each and every one of us, come such terrific storms of restlessness, such lightnings of anger or temper, such torturing hours of ennui, beside which the windless lifelessness of Sargasso is as activity. How fierce their resentment of that onward shift and push of life that eventually loosens each and every barque from its moorings and sets it adrift, rudderless, upon the great, uncharted sea, their eyes and their mood all too plainly show. And yet here they are, and here they will remain until their barque is at last adrift, the last stay worn to a frazzle, the last chain rusted to dust. And betimes they wait, the sirenic call of older and better days ever in their ears—those days that can never, never, never be again.

Who would not be ill at ease at times? Who not crotchety, weary, contemptuous, however much he might choose to possess himself in serenity? There is this material Snug Harbor for their bodies, to be sure. But where is the peaceful haven of the heart—on what shore, by what sea—a Snug Harbor for the soul?

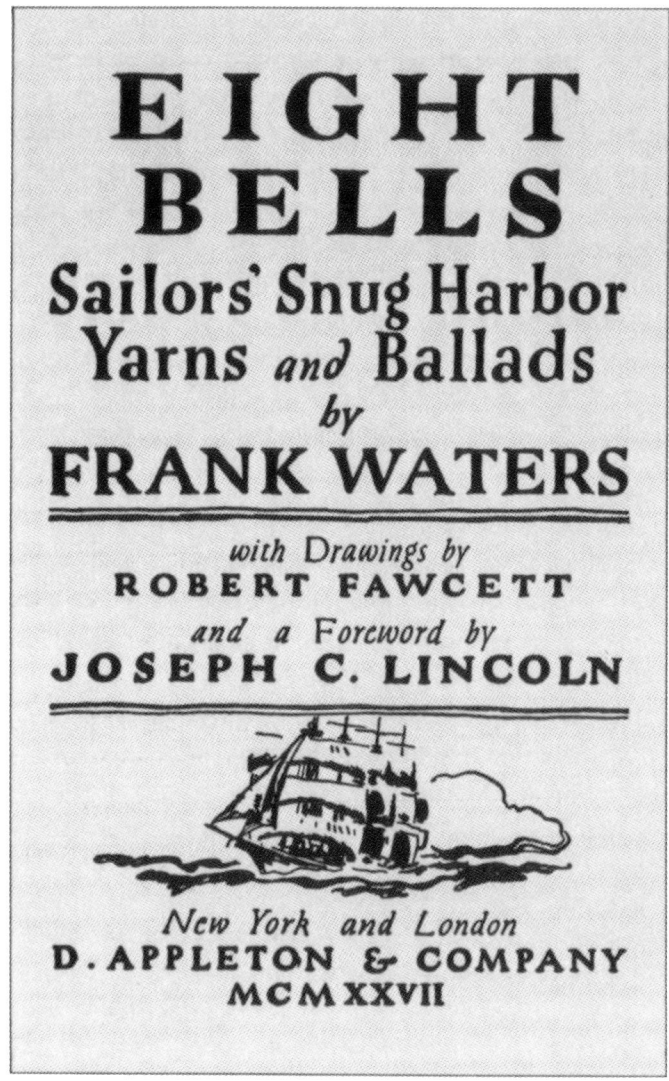

OLD CAP KNOWLES Unlimbers his Tongue an' Tells how he was Shanghaied

OLD MAN KNOWLES after unshipping his false teeth and stowing them away carefully in his starboard vest pocket, explaining to the old Snug Harbor salts that composed his audience, that before commencing to spin a yarn he usually removed the molars for fear that while speaking they might break away from their moorings and float around in his mouth impeding his speech or perhaps drift down his throat and choke him, settled himself comfortably in his seat and began to spin his yarn.

* * * * * *

"My maiden voyage at sea was on board of a Whaler in the years of eighteen hundred and fifty five, fifty six, and fifty seven, sailing from New Bedford—my home town—in the month of March fifty five and returning back to that port in October eighteen hundred and fifty seven with the hold filled to the hatch combings with oil. That one voyage on an old greasy Whaler was enough of 'blubber hunting' for me, so after a couple of months at home I came on to New York intending to ship on a coasting vessel and remain on the coast, and had made up my mind that I would not ship on any craft bound offshore, for the present at any rate.

"Now I had lived in the fo'castle of that blubber hunter for over two years and had heard all sorts of yarns spun about crimping boarding masters and their runners and thought that I knew enough to cruise around the water fronts of any port without drifting into the clutches of Crimps and getting Shanghaied. Now what I thought I knew and what I did know were two different things. Instead of hanging around the shipping offices on West St where all the coasting skippers applied for sailors when in need of crews, like a haymaking Rube I drifted into the fourth ward, where all the deep water sailors' boarding-houses were, with rum-shops, free and easys, and dance halls, scattered promiscuous about and schools of the most vicious types of land sharks—sailor boarding-house crimps—swarming around eager and ever ready to pounce on their prey, a sailor, and Shanghai him on board of a deep water ship bound to hell for what they'd care, as long as they got for placing him on board drunk or sober, three months of his wages in advance and perhaps blood money besides."

Here old Cap paused to survey the weather-beaten mugs of the storm battered old Barnacle-backs that were listening, and stroking the foot or more of snow white beard that flowed from his chin and jaws, continued his yarn.

"You old whales have all made sundry pilgrimages to that once unholy section of the city that run fore and aft through the fourth ward, from Franklin Square on Cherry Hill, to Pike Street and beyond, and athawtships from Park Row, and the Bowery to the river front, known as New Yorks Sailor Town. And you all know that in the days when three months wages was advanced to sailors that shipped on a deep water vessel that the Crimps of New York—or other ports for that matter—would not hesitate to Shanghai a sailor, nor any one else that got into their clutches if there was a ship ready to sail and wanted a crew or part of a crew. I don't know if any of you were ever Shanghaied. I know I was and thousands of miles from New York before the Dead Horse was worked up, and I was done sweating for the Damned Crimp that Shanghaied me.

"Ye all know the 'Flags of all Nations,' the old dance hall that used to be on James St in the old days. One afternoon I was passing by that Joint when a fellow standing in the doorway hailed me and when I stopped he came out on the sidewalk and asked me if I was staying in a deep water boarding-house waiting for a chance to ship. I told him that I was not staying in a boarding-house because I did not want to go deep water, that I intended to ship on a coasting schooner if I could get a chance.

"'You want a chance to ship on a schooner, hey?' says he, 'Well its a good job I hailed you brother, I been hunting around in the free and easys, and dance halls to try and pick up a few coasting sailors, but all I could find in them joints were deep water men boarding in deep water boarding-houses, and their boarding masters of course would not let them ship on a coaster.'

"I asked him where the schooner lay, and where she was bound to. 'She's anchored at Red Hook loaded with coal and bound to Portland Maine,' says he. 'Where is your clothes? If you have any let's go and get them and I'll take you to the man that will ship you on the schooner.'

"Well that fellow's proposition looked good to me, and we went and got my dunnage out of the Old Slip Hotel where I roomed since coming to New York and he took me to a place on Water Street next door to where Gallus Liverpool Mag kept her notorious dump."

When the ho-ho's and hah-hah's of old Caps audience that were one and all formerly acquainted with that locality had subsided, Old Cap resumed where he was interrupted in his yarn by those that knew that no coasting sailors boarding-house could exist and thrive in that neighborhood.

"The Boss of that shebang where that fellow

took me said it was right, there was a berth for me on a two masted schooner if I wanted to make a coasting trip to Portland and back to New York and I told him it suited me. There was three other fellows in the house that he said were going on the same vessel and he then went into another room and brought out a bottle of whiskey and glasses and invited us all to drink and have a good time.

"Whatever sort of chain lightening dope was in that bottle soon done the trick, and when I again got sober enough to get my correct bearings, I found myself on board of a vessel outside Sandy-hook, not a two-masted schooner bound to Portland, but a three masted full rigged ship bound to Rangoon in the east Indies. My bag of clothes—just as I last packed it—was on board all right but not another scrap of anything (not even soap and matches for the voyage) to show for the Dead Horse I would have to work up, three months of my hard earned wages advanced to a damn Crimp I did not owe a cent to. I realized right away that I was Shanghaied, and cussed myself for a fool that didn't tumble to the fact that day in front of the Flags of all Nations dance hall, that the rooster that hailed me and rang in his bluff about the schooner was a Sailors Boarding-House Jackal."

Here old Cap again paused for a few moments and continued, "I dare say some of you old timers may have seen during your casual trips among the Dives on the Bowery, a Duck that had one ear off and a scar that run from his right cheek bone to his chin. Well if any of youse have seen him, I would have you know that he was the Jackal that steered me to the Crimp that Shanghaied me, and two years afterwards I had the luck to run afoul of him alone one night with no one around, and I promptly unshipped one of his lugs, and placed my brand upon his cheek."

Those that heard old Knowles spin his yarn had no doubts about him fixing that Jackal as he said he did, for it was well known ashore and afloat among men that knew him, or knew of him, that he was a dangerous man for a Crimp or other Crook to run up against with evil intent, as he was sure to avenge an injury done him if he ever come across the party that done it.

"Well," says old Cap going on with his yarn, "there was nothing to do but grin and bear it as it was not so hard to do on the Ship *Sultana* of Boston which was the ship's name and home port. The Skipper Captain Amos Snow, was a religious man that did not believe in the belaying pin Gospel of driving sailors nor would he allow the Mates to swear at the crew, nor the crew to swear at each-other. He would not permit any unnecessary work to be done on sundays and if the weather was fine he would invite all that wanted to come aft to hear him read the Bible, to do so.

"Now there was an Irishman named Paddy Mullins on board which some of you might know. Some of the fellows in the crew that knew Paddy ashore in New York, said that he always hung out in Branagins rum mill day and night and was never sober. Every sunday that the skipper had his prayer meeting aft, Paddy was sure to be there, and when a hymn was sung he would throw his head back and chest out, and join in the chorus roaring and bellowing as if it was a heaving chanty on a windlass he was singing. Of course us fellows forrard in the fo'castle did not know what to think about Paddy, whether he was shamming and went aft to the prayer meetings to curry favor with the skipper, or whether he was in earnest and had seen the errors of his past life and was getting converted.

"Paddy was as ignorant as a bull's foot and could neither read or write, so when one day while steering my trick at the wheel and the skipper asked me if I would do him a favor by reading a chapter of the New Testament and explain it to Paddy during our watch below every day (we were both in the same watch) I told him I would do so. From then until we arrived at Rangoon I would spend a half of an hour, some days an hour of my watch below when I should be sleeping, or doing something for myself, in reading the Bible and trying to hammer in to Paddy's thick head the meaning of what I read. Paddy would sit with hands clasped and eyes rolled up until the pupils were hidden beneath the lids listening to me and when I was finished Paddy would sigh and murmur, 'Ah, God will bless you for leading one of his lost lambs back to the fold,' though somehow I never could stretch my imagination far enough to picture that Hyenna as a lamb, and sure enough I was right as we all learned soon after making Rangoon.

"I suppose you all have heard about the Elephants—if you aint been there to see—working in the dock yards at Rangoon carrying and piling heavy teak timber. If any of you have been to either Maulmein or Rangoon, you must have seen the Elephants working. I seen as many as a dozen Elephants picking up great square logs of teakwood some times one Elephant to a log sometimes two Elephants to a log, and carrying them some distance and stacking them up in piles ten or twelve feet high, as neat and straight as men could pile them.

"There was one Elephant that carried a piece of heavy chain three or four feet long with his trunk. That Elephant was the Boss and if any of the others tried to loaf on the job he would wade in to them and give them a hammering with the chain. The coolie Boss just pointed out the logs to be shifted and where to be taken and piled, and just stood back and the old Elephant with the chain would see that it was done pronto. Them Elephants would not turn to and work one second before the bell rang at the proper time and if two or one of them were carrying logs and come to where they were going to place them on the pile, if the bell happened to ring for knocking off time before they put them on the pile, they would drop the logs right on the ground and start for their quarters at once. If the Coolies tried to rob them of their proper allowance of food or stole any of their arrack and added water to it to make up for that they stole, when the bell rang for them to go to work again they would not turn to until they got their full whack of grub, and full share of arrack—or rum.

"When we were at Rangoon in the ship *Sultana* there was a very old Elephant that had worked many years in the dock-yard carrying and piling timber, which the Government pensioned off and allowed to wander around and go where it pleased about the place. For some years before the time we were there and many years after, that old Elephant would be at the boat landing every morning early waiting for the ship's boats to come ashore with sailors that were going on liberty. All the crews of ships that come to Rangoon knew about the old Elephant and were not surprised when the old animal joined the first gang that come on shore on liberty and went with them to the grog shops that sailors were bound to steer for as soon as they landed. The old Elephant expected his share of booze and the sailors would buy buckets of arrack and give it to him. It was a common sight most any afternoon in Rangoon to see a gang of drunken sailors, and the old Elephant as drunk as any of them, staggering along toward the Esplanade, where later on they could be seen laying about on the grass having a snooze with the Old Elephant stretched out in the middle.

"We were only a few days in Rangoon when Paddy Mullins persuaded the Old Man to let him have fifty rupees—a rupee was worth about fifty cents then—to send to his Mother in Ireland. Now the skipper believed that Paddy was converted, so he let him have the money and let him go ashore for the day to see about sending the money home. Now that day and night passed and Paddy did not come on board, and the next day and night passed and he did not show up. On the third day a Policeman came on board of the ship with the news that Paddy was in the Calaboose, and the Old Elephant was in jail too. That is they had him chained up in a yard back of the Police compound.

"It appears from what we on board of the Ship heard that Paddy when he got on shore that day forgot all about prayer meetings and Bible classes when he hove to in the first rum joint he arrived at and began to guzzle booze. He was not long there before a bunch of fellows ashore on liberty from one of the ships in port hove in sight steering a course direct for the same rum shop, with the old Bum Elephant following in their wake. Paddy joined the gang and that afternoon they were all gloriously drunk, Elephant and all of them together steering a zig zag course for the Esplanade. The next morning after that crowd sobered up a bit and went on board of their ship, Paddy and the old Elephant who by then were quite chummy together, the Elephant perhaps not forgetting that Paddy gave him a few buckets of arrack the day before, after waiting a while at the landing and no signs of another boat with a liberty gang showing up, started off on a spree by themselves. That tricky Irishman you can bet did not blow in all his rupees the day before and had a few shots left in his locker yet.

"Well Paddy and the Elephant got uproariously drunk and instead of shaping for the Esplanade to have a snooze and sober up they staggered along until they came to the gate leading in to the hansomest gardens in all Burma belonging to Sir Ramagee Framagee a very rich Parsee and at that time the chief Magistrate of Rangoon. When the Parsee Nabob looking out of his library window, seen a drunken sailor and a drunken Elephant staggering and floundering about among his beautiful flower beds leaving wrack and ruin in their wake as they lurched across beds containing the rarest of plants, he dove out of the window and roared for help as he grabbed a near by garden fork and charged the Elephant.

"As we heard the story Paddy and the Elephant were near an artificial lake when Ramagee Framagee came bearing down on them with the pitch fork ready for action, and as soon as he got within range the old Elephant grabbed him with his trunk and threw him in the lake. Well the upshot of the affair was that about a hundred of the Parsee's servants when they heard old Ramagee yelling for help, came to his rescue, and after pulling him out of the lake they grabbed Paddy, and drove the old Elephant in to a barn, where he was kept until nearly a regiment of sepoys came to take the both of them to jail.

"Well in the end Paddy was tried before old Ramagee Framagee himself who give him one year's hard labor in Jail. The skipper was disgusted with Paddy and glad to be rid of him. As for myself when I thought about all them hours in my watches below that I spent reading the Bible to Paddy, and when I remembered how he referred to himself as a lost lamb being led back safe to the fold, I says to myself a lamb, a poor stray lamb indeed, Why the damn Pole Cat,—that's what he is instead of a lamb—I am only sorry that he did not get sentenced to Prison for life, if for nothing else only for getting that poor old Bum Elephant in jail. When our cargo was discharged we sailed in ballast to Calcutta where we loaded a general cargo for New York all hands that left New York in the vessel returning on her excepting Paddy Mullins the holy Joe hypocrite."

* * * * * *

GAFF TOPSAIL BEN BREEZE
Tells about the Frescoing of Clam Quinn

BEN BREEZE nicknamed "Gaff Topsail" Ben, not alone for the shape of the extraordinary long nose that adorned his face and somewhat resembled a gaff topsail by its shape, but also for a rumour that was current among mariners forty years ago that Ben while once on board of a schooner laying at Baltimore could not get any money that was due him, and in order to "raise the wind" to go ashore and have a spree he arranged with a Junkman to bring his boat under the schooners bow one night and he sold one of the vessels gaff topsails to the Junkman. Ben was arrested and done six months in jail for that little affair but the news circulated and for years on the coast and deep-water he was known as "Gaff Topsail" Ben.

* * * * * *

"There's some good old Timers planted up there on Monkey Hill and when I slip my cable I expect to fetch up there myself. The old Snugs that christened the cemetary 'Monkey Hill' didn't make any mistake by any means when they gave the boneyard at Snug Harbor that name. Any lad that started to sea on a Wind Jammer, and for years stuck to the same, done enough climbing on ropes and spars to rate as a monkey, and the reason that some sailors I have known couldn't outclimb any monkey that ever come out of a jungle was their lack of a tail."

Thus Gaff Topsail Ben Breeze began to orate to entertain a group of old seadogs like himself, one summer afternoon while they smoked their pipes as they sat on the benches 'neath the shade trees on Sailors Snug Harbor grounds. "As I was saying," continued Ben, "there's some good old Timers stowed away for keeps over there on Monkey Hill, and among them old Timers are some old shipmates of mine of whom I could spin some pretty good yarns but none perhaps more amusing than the yarn I am now going to spin about him who we planted this morning on Monkey Hill, Clam Quinn, who ye all know well.

"Ye all know that during the Civil War there was a lot of Merchant sailors joined the Yankee Navy and I was one of them that joined and remained in the outfit a few years after the close of the war. In eighteen hundred and seventy one I went out from the cob dock in the U.S. transport *Supply* with a draft of men to relieve the crew of the *U. S. S. Lancaster* then Flag Ship on the south Atlantic station. The *Lancaster* was laying at Rio de Janerio when we arrived at that port and the next day we exchanged, we that came out in the draft going on board of the Flag Ship with our bags and hammocks, those on the *Lancaster* whose three year term had expired (or would at about the time they reached the United States) taking our places on the *Supply*.

"Well, Clam was in that draft and him and I were shipmates on the *Lancaster,* and the planting of him this morning reminds me of a scrape that he got into at Rio where-in he created an uproar of laughter fore and aft throughout the ship, though that among some of the officers was mingled with indignation, particularly the officer of the deck at the time that Clam pulled off his stunt. Clam was not alone in the affair that caused the uproar on board of the ship that evening—it was just four bells six o'clock when it happened—and his chum who was rated as a landsman on board and claimed to be an ex-professor of the Dublin University was just as queer a character as himself.

"Julian Ambrose Doyle—that smelt like a Purser's name to me—and Clam Quinn went ashore in Rio on twenty four hours liberty and when the time to report on board arrived they did not show up. When they did not show up in three or four days and none of the men that were ashore on liberty during that time had run into them it was believed that they had deserted. One evening just after four bells had struck the quartermaster on duty reported to the officer of the deck that a shore boat was coming alongside of the starboard gangway with an officer in a Brazilian Naval Captain's uniform sitting in the sternsheets. The Lieutenant that had charge of the deck ordered the orderly on duty at the cabin door to report to the Captain that a Brazilian Naval Captain was coming aboard, and ordered side boys to the gangway and a Boatswain's mate to pipe the Brazilian Captain over the ship's side. The Captain of the ship—a four striper—and the first Lieutenant stood on the starboard side of the quarter deck to receive the distinguished visitor and the officer of the deck stood just inside the gangway to salute him when he came on board.

"The boat came alongside and the Bo'sun's mate began to pipe on his call when lo and behold who marches over the gang-way, none other than Professor Julian Ambrose Doyle, rigged out in a Brazilian Naval Captain's uniform and following in his wake came Clam Quinn, with nary a stitch of clothes on him but a piece of grass matting that reached from his hips to about a quarter of the way to his knees and he tattooed or painted from his chin to his toes on every inch of his carcase that was visible with all kinds of pictures and curlicues in red and blue colors. Both had a good jag on but that did not prevent them from saluting the flabbergasted officer of the deck who for a moment or two was speechless with amazement. When he did get his speech that Luff made use of it good and plenty to tell that pair what he thought of them and wound up by roaring out to the Corporal of the guard and Jimmy Legs—master-at-arms—to clap double irons on to them and put them in the Brig.

"By that time the gangways were crowded with Blue Jackets and Marines roaring with laughter, and though the Skipper and executive officer, and Lieutenant that was at the gangway to receive the Brazilian Captain with the honor his rate entitled him to may not have enjoyed it over much, I'll bet my whack of duff for a month that when the news was spread through the Ward-room and steerage among the commissioned and non-commissioned officers how Professor Doyle and Clam Quinn was received over the gangway with honors due Naval Captains that there was laughing aplenty, not only then but many times after when ever the incident was recalled to their minds.

"After being confined in the Brig—in irons—for a week or more Clam and Doyle were brought to the Mast where the first Luff give them a call down telling them that they should be tried by a court-martial and punished. However they did not get a court-martial trial—either general or summary—but were returned to duty with the understanding that for one year they would be on the Black-List deprived of liberty to go on shore and of receiving any liberty money from the Purser, besides they would be detailed during that period to perform various disagreeable tasks assigned to them especially during time that the rest of the ships company were at leasure. When they were dismissed from the mast and came forrard Professor Doyle told the story of their adventure ashore describing in detail what led up to him appearing over the gang-way in a Brazilian Naval Captains uniform, and Clam Quinn in the rig of a South Sea island cannabal.

"It appeared according to the Professors yarn that when they awoke in the morning after they had come ashore the day before and started on a roaring spree, when they come to over-haul their pockets and Monk-bags (small bags that old time Navy sailors wore hanging inside their shirts from a string around their necks, in which they kept their money) they found that all they had between them was four millreis and a few copper dumps, a dump being worth about two cents American money.

In wandering about Rio they day before they drifted on to a piece of ground where there was a small circus performing in a tent, and some small side shows exibitting wax figures and freaks. They took a look at all there was to be seen and in the tent where the freaks were Doyle noticed that one attraction that usualy is among the collection of freaks in shows of that kind was missing. Now Julian Ambrose Doyle once being a Professor in a University was no slouch when it come to speaking foreign lingoes, and besides he at one time during his career—since booze had floated him out of a snug berth in a colledge and set him adrift like a direlict—had fetched up in Pernambuco where as a Beachcomber he learned to patter the Brazilian bat like a native.

"Now when Clam Quinn and himself awoke that morning and discovered that four millreis —about two dollars American money—and a few dumps represented their united capital— the Professor remembering the lack of a tattooed man among the freakes at the circus ground, hit upon an idea that appealed to Clam as well as himself to be a good way to raise the wind and have a good time on shore as long as they liked to stay. Now Professor Doyle knew something about drawing and painting, enough he told Clam to decorate his whole carcase with pictures and curlicues to exibit him in a show as a tattooed cannabal chief from the South Seas. He himself with his knowledge of the Brazilian lingoe was sure that he could do the barking that well that there would be a steady stream of visitors to view the tattooed ex-cannabal chief that in his island home had a collection of more than fifty heads that he had cut off from enemys he had killed and helped devour.

"When Clam heard Doyle explain his idea he agreed right away to join the Professor in his scheme to raise the wind and consented to have Doyle paint and decorate him from his hair to his toe nails with figures of fishes, birds, frogs, snakes and all the curlicues with which a Kanaka or Maori chief is tatooed with.

"Well as Doyle spun his yarn they was not long in getting under way and shaping a course to where they could buy the blue and red paint the Professor needed to decorate Clam with. After getting the paint and small brushes they dropped in to a booze shop to get a drink and there they run into a Brazilian fellow that Doyle knew when he was Beachcombing in Pernambuco, who had a room upstairs above the booze shop rented, and after having a few drinks together the three went upstairs to the Brazilians room where Doyle told his scheme to the Brazilian who agreed that it was O.K. He told Doyle and Clam that his cousin owned a building right across the street from where the circus tent was pitched and that there was a good sized vacant store on the ground floor that would be a good stand to exibit Clam in and he was sure that his cousin would let him occupy it free of charge for a short time. Clam and the Professor agreed to give the Brazilian a third of the profits and he told them to make themselves at home in his room while he went to see his cousin and get the key of the store from him.

"Now Clam Quinn though an American of Irish descent had a hide on him as brown as a Kanakas and did not need to be stained with coffee before decorating it. When the Brazilian had gone Clam shed all his raiment until stripped to bare poles, then the Professor got busy with paint and brushes and agin the time the Brazilian got back he had Clam frescoed from scalp to toenails, transmogrified into as fierce a looking cannabal chief as ever smacked his lips after eating the heart of an enemy or picking his thigh bone clean on one of the Pacific islands. When the Brazilian got back he gaped with amazement when he spotted Clam in his new rig. All that was needed to complete Clams attire was a yard and a half of straw matting to tie around his waist so as to reach about a foot below his hips.

"Of course every day before going on exibition Clams picture gallery had to be touched up here and there with fresh color, but upon the whole Professor Julian Ambrose Doyle's effort as an artist was a success that he was proud of. They next got several yards of white duck canvass which the Brazilian paid for and Doyle painted a picture representing an island in the South Seas, with a cannabal chief standing on the shore. That was to hang up in front of the store where Clam was to be exibitted and they were then ready to open the show and collect the shekels from all and sundry that Professor Doyles barking in Brazilian lingoe could attract and persuade to enter.

"Well as Doyle stated their exibition from the beginning was a howling success, yes howling thats the word right enough. When the store became crowded so as no space remained vacant for others to get in Clam would grin and grind his teeth and let out several most unearthly howls as he leaped around on the large heavy table that they borrowed from a Butcher in the next shop which done nicely for a stage, and when he seen some of the timid ones edging toward the door he would roll his eyes about and let out an extra bloodcurdling yell that would frighten the whole audience that would make a stampede for the door, and make room for others to get in. Yes, a howling success thats the right name for it all right.

"As the Professor remarked they were launched and on the right tack and were forging ahead on the tide of success, when one afternoon who should drift into the show but a bunch of young Naval officers belonging to the Brazilian Navy. One of them knew the Brazilian that was in partnership with Doyle and Clam, and he proposed that they should attend a party he was giving at his fathers house the following night and to bring the Cannabal chief with them to exibit to his friends. He told them that to make it more interesting that he would steal a complete Brazilian Captain's Naval uniform from his uncle's wardrobe—his uncle was a Naval Captain—for Professor Doyle to wear at the party to give the guests at the Party the impression that Doyle was a naval captain that had captured the cannabal chief on a recent voyage among the South Sea islands. He told them he would send the uniform to their room the next forenoon and call for them with a coach to take them to the party in the evening.

"Well according to Doyles yarn, about ten oclock the next forenoon the uniform was brought to their lodgings and the Professor put it on and it fitted him to a tee. The Professor touched up the frescoing on Clam's carcase with a fresh coat of paint and at three oclock every bit of it looked fine and dry. About four oclock the coach with the Brazilian's friend in it arrived and the three of them boarded the coach which started off. After a while they pulled up at a place where they were received by several other young fellows in Naval uniform. The drinks were passed around soon after they entered the house and continued to be passed around in quick succession until the first thing Clam and Doyle knew they knew nothing but were both hilarious drunk.

"In spinning his yarn Doyle said that when he got sober and found himself in double irons in the Brig he knew what happened right enough. He said he then knew that their Brazilian Partner had rung in a slick bluff on Clam and him when he planned with the young Naval officer to get Clam and him good and drunk and then Shanghai them back on board of the American Flag-ship, one rigged out in a Brazilian Naval Captains uniform, the other dolled up in a suit of oil paintings that was painted on, and promiscuously strewn about his hide. What ever motive them Brazilians had in playing that trick on Doyle and Clam there was no intent to rob them, as Doyle had over two hundred millries in his monk-bag when he come to over-haul it when he got sober. Half of what he had of course belonged to Clam Quinn, as he played the star part in their show, while the Professor acted as general manager and treasurer and in good time he divided it with Clam.

"After being discharged from the Navy at the end of that cruise I shipped in the Merchant service and remained in that service for many years, until age and infirmities compelled me to drift into Snug Harbor where I run up against Clam Quinn for the first time since we were shipmates in the Navy. Several years after I joined the Merchant service I happened to be ashore in Sydney Austrailia one saturday night. I was second Mate of the ship *Akbar* belonging to Boston at the time and had come ashore that afternoon to take in the sights and enjoy myself intending to go on board of the ship the next morning. While cruising around I fetched up in the Albert Park and attracted by a crowd that was gathered around a speaker that stood on a stool—soap-box or something I sheered over toward the crowd to investigate. When I edged up close enough to get a good view of the speaker I was flabbergasted to behold Professor Julian Ambrose Doyle rigged up like a real Sky Pilot performing sleight of hand tricks with cards and other articles, and peddling a hair restorer which he claimed that he had discovered, guarrenteeing it to grow hair on a brick, or restore faded hair to its original color.

"When I hailed him and made myself known to him he tabbooed peddling for the rest of the day and grabbing his stool and grip holding his stock of magic hair restorer, led the way to the side door of a hotel near-by where we slaked our thirst and exchanged yarns about ourselves. He told me since leaving the Navy that he had been following numerous games ranging from temperance orator to thimble-rigger, sometimes living on easy street, sometimes bringing up in jail. I have never seen or heard of the Professor since that night I bid good bye to him in Sydney, but I guess where ever Professor Julian Ambrose Doyle fetched up he would claim and get the sort of easy living that he reckoned the world owed him."

So now begins my first sea voyage. Oh my, I thought I was going to heaven! I was out of my mind with excitement. I got an old wooden sailor's chest belonging to my mother's brother, Captain Charles Allen, and I spent my time until the ship was ready, packing my clothes in the chest and getting everything ready. They had to get me a pair of sea boots, oilcoat and pants, a blue knitted sailor's Guernsey, canvas jumper, a belt and sheath and knife. Then I was as proud as a peacock going around for two days wishing all my friends and relations good-by and my grandmother good-by. She was my mother's mother. She said, "Well, Will, if you make as good a sailor as any of your five uncles, you will be all right."

When I came to wish my mother and father good-by, poor mother hung on to me and cried but father said "good-by" and shoved me away from him. Mother gave me plenty of spending money, about twelve pounds, English money.

When we got outside of the Heads the ship began to jump and pitch about and it was not long before I was as sick as I could be. The Captain helped me down to the cabin and put me in the bunk. I was only eleven years old but you bet I was sick for about five days. Then I began to get better and I was able to get up on deck but I could not eat anything. I forgot to mention that whilst I was so seasick, the cook used to come in the room sometimes and say, "Billy, if you want to get well quick, get a small piece of fat pork with a string on it and swallow it, then haul it up again." That used to make me twice as sick as I was before. One day as he stood in the room door telling me this, the Captain came down and heard him, but the cook did not see the Captain until he got a sock on the jaw and it knocked him over. The Captain said, "You damned skunk, don't you think that boy is sick enough without trying to make him worse?"

Of course I was pretty seasick but when I got over that seasickness and got up on deck and got properly clear of it, I tell ye what, that old Captain had his heart in his throat all the time. I thought I was in heaven; I was away climbing aloft everywhere. I was like a bird, like a monkey around everything and out on the yard arm. Of course Morrissey, the Captain, he knew what I could do—he used to see me in port on the vessels—he knew there was no fear in me, but he'd roar out every now and then, "Billy, damn your soul, you're going to get overboard." I'd look down and laugh at him. I might be up there all day long, I'd be up and down, one mast to the other. I hadn't an ounce of fear in me. I used to go from one mast to the yard and then I'd start and go across the arm out onto the brace and that brace with my weight on it, when I'd get out in the middle, would be going up and down about a foot. In the evenings, in the dog watches, when the men wouldn't be doing any work, they'd be sitting around on the decks—both watches would be on the deck of a fine evening, sitting down. And do you think you could keep me clear of them? I was stuck right in the middle of them and I'd have my two ears cocked to hear everything that was said on either side and I'd swallow it. And then when I saw the Captain he'd say, "Now, look here, your father will give me fits. He told me to keep you clear of the sailors, not to let you learn any badness." "I'm learning no badness, Captain. Everything I hear is good. They are nice men and they all talk nice and I get a lot of information." "What information do you get?" he says. Says I, "They show me splices and describe everything." "Oh, well, that won't hurt you," he says. But he'd sooner not see me there; he knew darn well they used to swear. At that time, to tell ye the truth, I hadn't learnt to swear—I thought that was an awful thing. I used to look up at the sailors in sort of a half dread when they'd swear. And I didn't learn it, not for a long time; in fact, I never got broken into swearing until I got to be a man and got to be an officer—not even when I was before the mast I didn't learn it, but when I got to be an officer and got charge on me and the men weren't doing exactly what I liked, or some fellow would make a row with me or give me an argument, then the first thing that'd come out of me would be an oath. I got it tangled up in me and even now, no matter what decent company I'm in, I'm sure I can't check myself—it comes out of me especially if I'm excited, telling a story or anything. It comes out of me and I don't know it. I'm not committing a sin because I don't know I'm swearing, y'see? I know lots of people pass a remark and say, "That seems to be an illbred fellow; where was he dragged up or what kind of a family had he," and all that. Well I can assure you it was different. If my father heard me swearing, even when I was a man and did learn to swear, at the table sometimes if I went a little too far he'd say, "Will, remember where you're to, will you please? You're not in a broil in a brothel now and you're not aboard ship among a lot of blackguards. Keep decent while you're here anyway."

However, everything went along all right with a few gales of wind thrown in just to break the monotony of it until we got to the Line, that is, the Equator, then Neptune came over the bows and asked if there was any of his children on board to be baptized. The Captain told him there was two, a fellow called Jim Brown and myself. Of course I made myself scarce; I flew up aloft on the mast. So they started to shave the other fellow with tar and grease for lather and a piece of old rusty iron hoop jagged all over for a razor. He kicked and roared like a town bull. Then they dumped him in a tub of salt water and scrubbed him with corn brooms.

Now it was my turn. They called me to come down but I would not. Now Neptune himself, he was a terrible looking object to me—his head was nothing but a mass of white hair—it came down nearly to his knees and his whole body was covered with knives and daggers. He pointed a big revolver at me and said, "Immediately, or I will shoot you." That brought me down and they shaved me just the same as the other fellow. Then Neptune wished the Captain good-by and went out over the bows. The Captain said, "Now, go down in my room and wash yourself properly." One day after this I saw the revolver in the Captain's room and I said, "Captain, Neptune left his gun behind him." So I understood all.

Every day now while we were going through the sou'east trade winds, fine weather, I spent most of the day out on the flying jibboom end with a fishing line trying to catch dolphin, and I caught one now and then. Sometimes I would catch one with a grains—that is an iron with four prongs like a fork with a beard on the end of each so that it will hold on to the fish when you drive it in. A dolphin is about three or four feet long and when you catch it, and it is dying on the deck it is a very pretty sight to see. It changes into all kinds of colors like a rainbow.

We arrived in Pernambuco, Brazil, in thirty-five days and the cargo sold well and I had a great time. The consignee invited me out to his home to stay while we were there. He had two boys and a girl near about my age. He was an Englishman by the name of Saunders. Every day we were off in the wagon driving all over the country, going around through the sugar plantations, eating sugar and all kinds of fruit. When we left I had the cabin full of presents for my mother and father and a monkey, a parrot and a marmoset for myself. Going home it was coming on winter and we had very bad weather, nothing but gales of wind and seas mountains high but I was not seasick. I knocked about all the time. We shipped a heavy sea one day and it washed one man about the deck and broke his leg and the Captain had to fix it with splinters. After thirty-seven days we got to St. Johns all right with the loss of some sails and other things.

You know, I'll never forget the very first voyage we made when I got home. Of course I knew on the voyage, the Mate told some of the men and they repeated it to me, that my father told Morrissey to give me a damn good putting through. He said, "You put him through. I don't want him to go to sea," he says, "but he is determined to go. Put him through and keep him at it, make him work, do everything." So when I came home at the end of the voyage after my mother had given me a couple of kisses, my father shook hands with me, he wouldn't kiss me, I suppose he was ashamed of the act, but he looked at me sideways and he says, "Well, Will, how do you like the sea?" "Fine," I says, "Father, I'm delighted with it. Jingoes, I think it's grand."

I tell ye I was very fond of it and even now if I was young enough I'd go back to sea again. In fact now I'm half dreaming about it; I don't know but what I will be out yet. What I like about it most is that it's not humdrum—it's not monotonous—there's always some excitement—something to look forward to—you're going to get in port or there's a gale of wind coming and you're expecting to see some big sea come and do damage—some kind of excitement—it's all the time changing, see, from one day to the other, from one month to the other—changing of ports. You go to a port to-morrow that you were never to before. Then you're living in the thoughts of going to a big circus to-night and all that kind of thing. Now on shore, there's one darn thing all the time. A man sits down to his work and if he's a carpenter he's working over and over and over again—the plane and the chisel—aw, it's slow, there's no excitement in it. After the day's work he goes home, gets his tea, well that's all the excitement there is. Comes home and goes to bed, gets up in the morning and goes over the same work again. But every morning at sea we don't know what's coming before the middle of the day. It might be a fight on the ship's deck among the sailors; it might be a man's washed overboard; it might be that a man falls from aloft and is killed. Always there's something to look forward to. People in the country—I've often looked at them with scorn.

APPRENTICESHIP—"MIRANDA"

I went apprentice in a Liverpool ship called the "Miranda." I was then about fourteen and I stayed in her for about four years. The Captain's name was Wakeham. He hailed from Brixham, West of England. He was a hard case. All them old West of England captains were in them days.

Now I can tell ye going to sea in them days, sixty-five years ago, is not much like now. Then you had to be a whole man before you dared to ship as an able seaman on a sailing ship. If the mate or captain gave you any job to do with a piece of rope or wanted you to repair a sail and you could not do it, your wages would be cut down to five shillings a month. The pay out of St. Johns them days was three pounds or three pounds ten shillings a month according to the supply and demand for able seamen. There were two rates out of England, two pounds ten shillings to go east or to the tropics, a fine weather voyage, and three pounds and three pounds five shillings to go across the Atlantic. First mates received six or seven pounds and ten pounds to the captains. In Newfoundland it was pounds, shillings and pence first but at the time I was mate it was changed to twenty dollar, ten dollar, five dollar and dollar notes. There was a fifty cent piece, no twenty-five cent piece, but twenty cents, ten cents, five cents and one cent.

Once you got out to sea there was all kinds of work going on. Knotting, splicing, fitting the rigging and all kinds of fancy work such as cutting out small brass stars to go on the lanyard knots of the rigging; grafting and fancy handles for a set of new quarter deck buckets; sewing mats for the rigging; putting a point on one end and an eye on the other of the big tow line or hawser (this should be grafted with small nettles); painting, scraping, varnishing and all kinds of work.

The first thing in the morning at six they would start to wash the decks. You would have to fist a big holystone, another a squigee and the rest the brooms and rags. It all had to be finished at eight bells, that is eight o'clock. Then the other work begins. So you see it is not as the old woman said to another, "Well, Mrs. Brine, them sailors have easy and great times, haven't they? Sitting down on their sterns all day letting the wind blow them along."

The sailors on steamers these days are a lot different. There may be one now and then amongst them that has served in sailing ships and knows his business, but he will be a pretty old man. All the A. B.s, as they call themselves these days, can do is wash the boats with a bucket of sudgy mudgy and rags. If you called one to heave the lead you might get one out of a fo'c'sle of ten men that could do it or that would know the marks and deeps on it. The first thing they will say if you speak to them sometimes is, "Oh, I didn't come here for you to show me my work." I think they are pretty well right there because more than one-half of the officers don't know how to show them.

Enough of that, we will go back to the old sailing ships or "wind jammers," as the steamboat men call them.

Well, to carry on about the "Miranda." That Captain did put us through. There was another apprentice, John Warren was his name. We were bound to Brazil and when we got clear of the bad weather and into the nor'east trade winds and fine weather the Captain used to have the jolly boat taken off the boat skids and hung in the boat davits aft by the mizzen rigging over the side. Every morning after breakfast he would call out to the chief officer, "Where are them boys? Send them along here." When we would come aft, he would say, "Into that boat the pair of ye." We would get into the boat and he would sit in the stern. "Warren, come here near me. Take that hand lead and line in your hands and coil it up." He would watch him and if he did not coil it the right way, he had a piece of rope in his hand, and he would give poor Warren a cut of it on the backside saying, "Oh, you damned sodger." When Warren got it all right he would call out "heave," then the line would run out. When he thought proper he would call "stop." Warren then would stop the line and he would say, "What water have you got?" Warren would bawl out in a singing way, "by the deep 12" or perhaps "quarter less 12." Or "by the mark 13" or "and a half 13."

On the ship we have what we call the deep sea lead line and the hand lead. The hand lead is smaller and only used in shallow water going in or out of a harbor. On the deep sea lead line that's only marked every five fathom up to one hundred and twenty or one hundred and thirty fathom. For instance for twenty fathom it's two knots, for thirty fathom, three knots; forty fathom, four knots and one single knot in between for every five fathom—we are not so particular about one fathom. But on the hand lead it's generally marked up to twenty fathom. There are nine marks and eleven deeps, the marks are there but you have to guess the deeps yourself. One fathom we call a deep. At two fathom—a fathom is six feet—at two fathom there's a piece of leather, split, with two ends on it. At three fathom it's the same way—there's a piece of leather with three tails. Now four fathom is a deep; five fathom is a mark, a piece of white rag—usually a piece of linen or any white rag at five fathom. Six fathom is a deep; seven fathom is a mark—we generally put a piece of red bunting. The reason we use bunting is that in the night, when a man can't make out the color, he can feel it and he knows the feeling of bunting from cloth, see? So that's at seven. At eight fathom, that's a deep—no mark; nine fathom is a deep—no mark; ten fathom is a piece of leather with a round hole in it, a little piece of flat leather with a round hole at ten fathom. Eleven fathom is a deep and twelve fathom is a deep; thirteen fathom is a mark and we usually put a piece of navy blue woolen cloth at thirteen. Fourteen is a deep and fifteen is another piece of white rag—a piece of white rag at fifteen as well as at five. Sixteen is a deep again, no mark; seventeen is the same as at seven—a piece of red bunting. Then eighteen is a deep and nineteen is a deep and twenty is the same as the deep sea—two knots.

The old Captain could see and if Warren made a mistake in singing out he would get another cut on the hind quarters. "Oh, you lubber, you will never make a sailor, get out of it." Then, "Barnes, take that line and show that sodger." I would take the line but it would not be very long before I would get a cut on my hind quarters or perhaps before I was done, two or three cuts. "You are a damned sight worse than that other sodger. Give him the line and get for'ard, you damned lubber. I'll never make a sailor of you." Well, he would keep us there for about a half hour pulling that line in and out. Then he would give us a parting cut each with, "Get to hell out, you damned greenhorns." The man at the wheel would be grinning at us.

The Mate would then set me cleaning the brass work around the wheel and hoops of the buckets on the poop deck. Warren would go below, he was in the Second Mate's watch; I was in the Mate's watch. There is always one watch below and the other on deck. The watches are four hours up and down but so that you would not have the same watch on deck all the time, they split the evening watch from four to eight, two hours each and call them dog watches.

Our Captain was a great man to carry sail until the last minute. If a squall was rising he would not start a rope till the squall struck her, then everything was flying together. In a squall or any other time our job was to go up to the top of the mast and make fast the sail called the royal. After the squall had passed on sometimes I would just be getting on the deck from the rigging when it would be, "Loose the royal and set it again and other light sails as well." I would have to mount the rigging again and loose it.

We lived in a fore cabin next to the cabin; it was called the half deck but we had a separate door to go into it. The sailmaker and carpenter lived there also. The four of us always had to dress in our best on Sundays and go to dinner in the cabin with the Captain and Mates. That was what we liked because we got a good blow-out of plum pudding with plenty of currants and raisins in it.

I won't forget that passage while I live. It was all calms and light winds. We were about seventy-five days getting to about three hundred miles from Queenstown. Then we ran right into a calm that had been there for about a month. Ships that had come along from all parts of the world for the last month had all accumulated there; large iron ships that had been out from home the last year, some two years, had barnacles, grass and conchs on their bottoms. It would take half a gale of wind to move one of them. Now our ship was wooden with copper on her bottom and although the others would not move we were worming along all the time, a quarter of a mile, sometimes a half a mile an hour. As we passed each ship their boat would come alongside and say they were starving. We were about seventy-five days out ourselves and short on allowances. We were living on rice, everything else was gone and the rice would not last much longer. We had only about a half a meal a day and about two small dippers of water a day. All we could give them was sugar—we had a cargo of that. Some ships we would give three bags to and others four and five, according to their size and number of men. The Captain said he could not see them starving and that some one would pay for it. After we had been in the calm for about a week steamers were sent out loaded with provisions to supply the ships.

A fine fair wind sprung up at last and we all started up the Channel and got into Queenstown two days after. We were all like skeletons but we had a square blow-out as soon as we were anchored. We laid there a week and were ordered to Bristol.

We were at Bristol, England, for ten days, that was our lay days for orders. It was late in November and when we left Bristol for St. Johns the gales of nor'west winds were settling in. We had a whole new crew shipped there and most of them had just left a ship from the East Indies and were warm weather sailors. We used to call them "South Spainers" them days. Well, Gentlemen, Sirs, we got it well cooked for us that passage. We had scarcely got clear of the Channel when it started in. When we were five days out we got an awful gale, in fact it was a hurricane. A sea struck her about noon and smashed up the two boats on the top of the fo'c'sle or crew's house and stove part of the starboard side of it in, filled the fo'c'sle, washing the watch below out of their bunks. Half their clothes went overboard and every movable thing about the deck. The galley was in the fore end of this house and it took the old nigger cook out. He was picked up away aft against the break of the poop.

Every day it would be blowing a gale and we would be shortened and reefed down to lower sails. Sometimes the wind would shift around to east or sou'east and we would have a fair wind and get two or three hundred miles along on our course. Then around it would go again and blow another gale which would drive us back the half nearly of what we made. Oh, it was heart-breaking. This new crew they were not used to weather like this; they were freezing and wet all the time. We had no way to dry our clothes, never got a fine day. Every time it would blow one or other of the sails would be blown away. We were all down in the cabin repairing the sails that had burst or torn. It was no nice job trying to sew heavy wet

canvas. We had to make a sail loft out of the cabin and the cabin skylight had to be boarded up to keep the sea from smashing the glass. We had to work by the anchor light and other lamps. It was miserable.

At last we got on the Newfoundland Bank, three hundred miles from St. Johns on the seventy-fifth day from Bristol. Now we had the worst part to go through—snow and frost. When we would go aloft to make a sail fast it would be frozen so hard that you could hardly bend it. You could not work with mitts on; you had to take them off before you went up in the rigging; you could not hold on with them as they would stick to the ice, and your hand would pull out—you would be sure to fall down and kill yourself or go overboard. We had got about halfway across the Banks when it came from the nor'west a terrible gale, the glass was down to twenty-eight. On the Banks, in a gale, an awful sea soon gets up which it did then. The next night at about eleven P.M. a terrible sea boarded her taking away the binnacle and compass, everything off the quarter deck or poop. It smashed in the cabin skylight and filled the cabin with water. It also took eighteen stanchions and all the bulwarks on the starboard side and whipped the jibboom out of her. It washed the starboard anchor off the bow where it was lashed with good strong chains and took it along to the forem'st where the flukes hooked in a spare spar that was well lashed to the deck. Two men went overboard from the fore end of the ship and the man at the wheel went with the compass and binnacle. I escaped the whole of it as it was my watch below at the time. All I wonder at is that it did not take the fo'c'sle house as well.

Now that all the damage was done there came a nice fair wind from the nor'west and we got to St. Johns three days after. I thought that passage from Bristol was a year.

My father knew all about the drubbing that we got; it was in the paper. He asked me how I liked the sea now. I said, "All right, I like it fine." He said no more.

He knew all about the sea. He could sail a ship himself and he told me how they were once chased off Cuba by a pirate and got clear of him. He said coming on night it got dirty and started to blow and rain. The pirate at dark was keeping right on after them. The old Captain of my father's ship was an Englishman by the name of Axtel. About ten in the night they could see the pirate's light and the Captain said to my father, "We have to loose our longboat, Sir," and he told him what he was going to do. My father approved of it. They got the longboat in the tackle and hung her out over the side with her mast standing up and put an anchor lamp on it. Out went all the lights except this one in the small boat. Then they hauled the ship on a right angle course and cut the boat adrift. In the morning no more pirate. Of course until daylight came they thought that light was the brig. Captain Axtel altered his course and steered east for a day then put her on her course for St. Johns again.

YELLOW FEVER—THE "RIVAL"

My first time as an officer was in the "Queen of Beauty" with old Captain Matty Dunn, he was called the "King of Ugly." I joined him as Second Mate and I can tell ye I was as proud as a peacock. My first voyage as Mate or Chief Officer was in the "Island Lass" when I was about twenty-one years of age.

Now the "Rival" was loading for Brazil. Her owners told me that Mr. Norris, the First Mate, was going to Halifax to take his examination for captain and that if I liked I could go in his place. Now the yellow fever was very bad in Brazil at this time, several of our captains and men had died of it and I believe that Norris was frightened to go down there so made the examination an excuse to get out of it. My mother and father did not want me to go but I should and would.

The Captain of the "Rival," George Branscombe, was a second cousin of mine and he had been master of my father's ship, the "Undine," before my father failed. He was a very nice man and I liked him very much.

We sailed for Pernambuco and had a very good passage, thirty-five days. We were ordered on to Bahia. The fever was very bad there then, some ships laying in the harbor with all hands gone, others with half the crew dead. We were five days getting to Bahia and we began to discharge the cargo. In those days the crews had to work the cargoes out of the ship. About the middle of the first day one man on the starboard winch handle gave out. The Captain was on shore, but he had ordered me if anyone got sick to hoist the yellow flag at once. I hoisted it up and the hospital boat came alongside and took him away. The next day another one gave up. We did the same with him. Two days more and a third gave up. We sent him ashore also. The hospital boat was kept busy going from one ship to the other all day long.

We got the last of the cargo out. As we did not have a charter yet I had the men employed at sundry jobs about the deck. I mixed a pot of paint and was painting when I felt awful sick. I stopped and went aft and sat down on the fore end of the cabin house. I was getting worse all the time, I knew it was the fever. I felt just the same as the others, pains in the back of the neck and calves, cold chills, perspiration, pulse racing, temples throbbing and feverish all over. When the Captain came aboard I told him I felt very bad.

He said, "Show me your tongue," and he felt my pulse. "Well, boy, I believe you have the fever. The best thing is to go to the hospital."

We hoisted the yellow flag and the boat came off and took me to the hospital. Branscombe was a fine fellow; he used to come up to that hospital to see us every day while we were there. One of us never came out, he died. I was delirious for several days and did not know Branscombe. He told me one day I went for him and said he was trying to get inside of me with my girl.

We got better but there was a great number died, I think about forty, while I was in there. There was a fine young man in the next bed to mine, he was Mate of a French bark. He had been bad but he was getting better too and he and I got to be great chums. We were allowed to go out on the veranda and sit there. He was a good hand to play the accordion and I used to be able to sing very well.

The interpreter at the hospital was a well-educated man. He had been an officer in the Brazilian army during their war with Paraguay and he had two beautiful daughters. He lived in the other end of the hospital—there was just a rail dividing his veranda from ours. The French Mate and I dragged our seats up alongside of the rail and these girls would come out and they got acquainted with us. The best-looking of the two was head and heels in love with this French Mate. I know she was—anybody could see that. I liked the other one myself. Sometimes the old man would come out and chase them in. One Sunday morning the French Mate and I were sitting there talking and playing. This was about ten o'clock. All at once he took bad.

I said, "Go in and lay down. Perhaps you're doing too much, you're not strong; you're starved to death, you know."

That's what they do, starve you right down to kill the fever. I'd have ate a dead horse if it came across me at the time. My God, I'd have ate anything, a dead man if I could have got hold of one as long as he was cooked.

The French Mate went in.

I sat there for an hour or two, trying to play on his accordion—I didn't know how to play then, but since then I've learned. A porter came out. This fellow couldn't speak much English. I says, "Where's my friend?"

"Oh," he says, "very bad. I tink he die."

"What?" says I.

I went in. I knew he wasn't dead, but he was delirious—he didn't know me. I was sorry. I went out and sat down. Then I went for a walk around the garden and over to the big shed—I never was in there before. "I wonder what's in there," I says. I saw the door open and I looked in, it was piled up tier after tier, full of coffins—they were lead color. They always had carpenters making these coffins when an epidemic broke out. I didn't want to look at that too long, I can tell ye, so I came out and went and laid down on my bed,

In the evening I went out again. It was about four o'clock and I saw the porters running in and out and I asked one of them what was the matter.

"Oh," he says, "friend die, he go, go, die."

Good God, I never got such a turn—I nearly got sick again myself.

Then I saw them going in with a coffin, and in about half an hour they brought out the coffin and a hearse came. They had to bring him down and around the end of the hospital, so I followed them. They took him up and put him on the hearse. There was no funeral, you know, only the fellow who was driving was dressed up in a uniform. When the coffin was lashed on the hearse they gave the horse a crack and away went the horse full gallop up the road. That was the last of the poor French Mate. He had died off quick with black vomit, a second relapse. I cried for him that night. I was as sorry as though my own brother had died.

I hung around for a few days. I was calling for something to eat all the time. "Oh, no, no, no, no," said the doctor. When the doctor came this morning I wanted him to let me leave the hospital.

I says, "I want to go out. I'm not sick now."

"Oh, no," he says, "I'll tell you when to go."

The next morning I got up, got my walking stick and came down around the garden. I had it all cut and dried, what I was going to do. I'd been down there before looking at that nice white sand. I strolled about a bit first and went down there gradually. They couldn't see me from the hospital on account of the trees. It was a beautiful garden full of trees for about one hundred and fifty yards and then a stone wall about ten feet high from the garden to the sand. I sat down on the wall and threw my stick over. Then I got out over the wall and hung down the full length of my arms and dropped. Another time I would have landed right on my feet, but I was that weak now that I fell on my hind quarters. I laid for a bit and got my breath, but soon got up and pointed her for town along the beach. All I had on was a white calico skull cap and a long white gown that came down to my slippers, the hospital convalescent rig. Around eleven o'clock, the sun began to get stronger and the sand was as hot as blazes under my feet. My slippers were the kind that had no heels in them. Every two or three steps the slipper would come off and I'd have to stop and put it on. I walked along, anyhow. I had to go what I suppose in the city would be three miles and I had to walk about a mile and three-quarters along the beach before I came to any of the wharves.

When I got down that far, I couldn't go any further along the beach. I had to go up on the street. Every one that passed me would stand and look after me, but I traveled along minding no one,—I was pretty tired by this time. I saw them watching me, but I wouldn't slew my head to look at any of them. I made tracks for the ship chandler's store. I walked pretty nearly through half the city before I got to Wilson's store. As the people went by they'd fly away out about ten yards from the side of the road till they got past me. I was yellow in the face and I scared every one, they didn't know what to make of me,—thought I must have been a madman out of a lunatic asylum; either that, or they knew I'd come out of the hospital. They couldn't make head nor tail of me at all.

I reached the ship chandler's anyhow and I bolted in the door. George Wilson himself was in back of the counter and the place was all open. All the ships' captains hung out about the ship chandler's because he had card tables and a billiard table and inside a nice parlor for the captains to sit and spend their time. Well, when they saw me come in several of them stood up—they didn't know what the hell it was. Wilson looked at me.

He says, "Good God, is that you, Mr. Barnes?"

"Yes," says I.

He says, "Did they let you come out of the hospital that way?"

"No," says I, "I came out. I wasn't going to stay there any longer, I wanted to come out two days ago." I says, "This morning I started down the gardens, got down on the shore and walked down the sandy beach."

"What," says he, "in all the hot sun?"

"Yes," says I, "and then I walked down through the town here."

"Good God," he says, "there's going to be murder about this! There's going to be hell to pay." He says, "Go in back there."

As I was going in back every son-of-a-bitch of them captains jumped up. One fellow looked at his watch—he had somewhere to go. Another had some other place to go and before you could say "knife" there wasn't a man at one of those tables, they had all cleared out. I suppose they were afraid they might take the fever from me. Wilson told me not to come out.

He says, "The Captain will be in here directly."

By and by in came Branscombe. He stood and looked.

"Hell," he says, "did they send you out of the hospital that way?" Those was the first words he said.

"No, I wasn't going to stay there," I says, "to starve. I was starving to death."

"There's going to be the devil to pay," says he. "What are we going to do?"

"There's a lot of old clothes in there," says Wilson, "come in."

We all went in and he opened a box and threw out an old sailor's reefing jacket, a skull cap and some boots and an old pair of pants. I pulled up the shirt that was on me and tied it around my waist, and fastened a cord around that and hauled on the old pair of pants that belonged to a sailor who was dead, I suppose. I was a hard-looking ticket. I'd have sooner kept on the hospital rig.

"Better bring him down and get him aboard as quick as you can before the doctor comes in and catches him here and yanks him back to the hospital," says Wilson.

I says, "I'll be damned if I'd go. I'd kill them if they tried to put me in the hospital again."

"Come on," says the Captain and he brought me down to the landing slip and called a boat. "Here," he says, "this is the Mate, take him out to the English brig 'Rival' and put him aboard. I'll pay you."

The fellow rowed me out and I got up the ladder. Old Scully, the cook, was in the galley for'ard. I didn't say a word, but I jumped right down the steps into the pantry. There was a big oval tureen half full of soup, they hadn't taken much out of it at dinner time. It was hot weather, you know, and they don't eat so much then. That cook knew how to make soup, too—with plenty of vegetables in it. I got the soup and I hadn't the patience to take a spoon, but I put the tureen up to my mouth and drank all that was in it. Then I looked in the locker and found a dish there with a lot of cold potatoes and cabbage and some fresh beets. I got them out; I didn't use a knife and fork, I went for it like a dog. God, I had good teeth in them days and I could grind it to pieces. I ate it all and when there was no more I went up on deck. Along about four or five o'clock I was as bad again as I ever was the first day I went ashore.

I said to the Second Mate, I says, "My God, I'm awful sick. I think I'll go and vomit."

I laid down again. The Captain came along about half-past five. He says, "What's the matter with you?"

"Oh, I'm sick again," says I.

"Christ," he says, "you had no business coming out of that hospital. There was hell to pay. The interpreter and the doctor came in after you left and they were raising hell in the store and they went for me. But," he says, "I had no trouble in quieting them, I had to grease their palms. I told them I'd let you stay aboard and if you got bad again I'd take you ashore. By God," he says, "I think you'll have to go again. You're bad now. You've taken a relapse."

However, I fell asleep and when I woke in the middle of the night I was all right. I had a smoke and the next morning I was as good as ever again. That was the end of that fever.

✺   ✺   ✺

And Now . . .

I WAS sitting in the Harbor the other day and, of course, there are a lot of old fellows around there, sitting about. Everybody is talking here and there—telling stories and spinning yarns. There is one old chap I know pretty well. We were sitting together.

"Well, Barnes," he says, "I don't suppose we'll be long for this life. You know we're getting pretty moldy now—we're into the eighties. Anyway, you look at it all around," he says, "you know damn well we haven't a hell of a lot more years, four or five anyhow."

I says "Four or five years is a hell of a long time; a man could make a fortune or two in four years."

"By God," he says, "I've given up all thoughts of that. The only thing I ever think of now," he says, "is my soul and the next world."

"Aw, go on with ye," I says, "thinking of yourself for the next world."

"Don't you ever think about the other world and dying?" he says.

I says, "No, I don't. In fact, it very seldom comes into my head," I says, "I'm so busy one way or another."

He began to get on his horns. He says, "Are you prepared to die?"

"Prepared?" says I. "I was always prepared. I've been prepared since tne first day I went to sea. When I thought the next moment I was going to be whipped into eternity, I wasn't afraid. If you don't know a sailor's religion, I'll tell it to you and this is my religion: a clear conscience, a sharp knife and ready to cut at a minute's notice."

Bibliography

Bills Paid, Sailors' Snug Harbor, 105 Vols., 1797-1905. MS. New York State University, Maritime College, Bronx, New York.

Trustees' Minute Books, 1806-1915. MS. Sailors' Snug Harbor, Sea Level, North Carolina.

Act of Incorporation and By-Laws of the Trustees of the Sailors' Snug Harbor [including Copy of the Last Will and Testament of Robert Richard Randall]. New York: William Mercein, 1819. Later editions with various addendums issued in 1842, 1848, 1876, 1883, 1900 and later.

"Sailors' Snug Harbor." *New York Evening Post*, October 29, 1831, p. 2.

"Sailors' Snug Harbor." *New York & Richmond County Free Press*, August 10, 1833, p. 115.

"Sailors' Snug Harbor." *The Sailor's Magazine and Naval Journal*, Vol. 6, September 1833, pp. 1-3.

"Institutions for Seamen." *The National Magazine*, Vol. 3, October 1853, p. 293.

W. W. Phillips, *Address Delivered at the Laying of the Corner-Stone of the New Chapel for the Use of the Inmates of the Sailors' Snug Harbor, On Staten Island*. New York: Edward O. Jenkins, 1855.

"Sailors' Snug Harbor Corner Stone of a New Chapel." *New York Daily Times*, November 22, 1855, p. 2.

W. W. Phillips. *Discourse Delivered at the Opening of the New Chapel Erected for the Inmates of the Sailors' Snug Harbor, On Staten Island*. New York: Robert Carter and Brothers, 1856.

"Sailors' Snug Harbor." *Harper's Weekly*, Vol. 11, August 31, 1867, pp. 351-52.

Louis Bagger, "The Sailors' Snug Harbor." *Harper's New Monthly Magazine*, Vol. 67, January 1873, pp. 186-197.

"Our Artist's Sketches at the Sailors' Snug Harbor." *The Daily Graphic*, September 2, 1873, p. 347.

Early Mayor's Papers, Charities, 1876-1897. MS. Municipal Archives and Record Center, 23 Park Row, New York City.

J. J. Clute, *Annals of Staten Island, From Its Discovery To the Present Time*. New York: Press of Chas. Vogt, 1877.

History of the Sailors' Snug Harbor Together with Incidents of a Life In It for Eighteen Months Written by an Inmate. Privately published: 1879.

"Sailors' Snug Harbor." Editorial, *Nautical Gazette*, November 2, 1882, p. 29.

"Sailors' Snug Harbor." *Harper's Weekly*, Vol. 26, August 12, 1882, p. 506.

Sailors' Snug Harbor, Investigation into Charges Preferred Against the Officers and Management. Report of Committee. New York: Slote & Janes, Stationers and Printers, Morse Building, 140 Nassau Street, 1883.

Franklin N. North. "Sailors' Snug Harbor." *Century Magazine*, Vol. 23, June 1884, pp. 192-201.

Charles J. Jones. *From the Forecastle to the Pulpit Fifty Years Among Sailors*. New York: 1884.

Illustrated Sketch Book of Staten Island, New York, Its Industries and Commerce. New York: S. C. Judson, 1886.

R. M. Bayles. *History of Staten Island From Discovery to Present*. New York: L. E. Preston Co., 1887.

"Sailors' Snug Harbor." *Harper's Weekly*, Vol. 34, March 29, 1980, p. 239.

Charles J. Jones. "Sailors' Snug Harbor, Staten Island." *Sailor's Magazine*, Vol. 64, March 1892, pp. 77, 78.

Mrs. R. F. Woodward. "The Sailors' Snug Harbor." *Frank Eslies Monthly*, Vol. 39, 1895, pp. 692-702.

Theodore Dreiser. "When the Sails Are Furled: Sailors' Snug Harbor." *Ainslee's*, Vol. 2, January 1899, pp. 593-601.

"Stories of the Sea." *Leslie's Weekly*, August 12, 1899, pp. 122-124.

"Delahanty Is Underfire, Nurse Alleges Intoxication." *New York Times*, November 12, 1899, p. 12.

"Trask Refuses Re-Nomination." *New York Times*, December 11, 1900, p. 3.

Ira K. Morris. *Morris's Memorial History of Staten Island*. New York: 1900.

Theodore Dreiser. "Sailors' Snug Harbor Home for Aged Skippers." *The Sunday Magazine New-York Tribune*, May 22, 1904, pp. 3-5, 19.

G. Richardson. "Sailors' Snug Harbor at Staten Island." *The Independent*, Vol. 65, November 20, 1908, pp. 1217-1220.

I. N. Phelps Stokes. *The Iconography of Manhattan Island, 1498-1909*, 6 vols. New York: Robert H. Dodd, 1915.

"When Sailors Come Home From the Sea." *New York Tribune*, November 26, 1916.

Charles Gilbert Hine and William T. Davis. *Legends, Stories and Folklore of Old Staten Island, Part I North Shore*. New York: Staten Island Historical Society, 1925.

Frank Waters. *Eight Bells: Sailors' Snug Harbor Yarns and Ballads*. New York and London: D. Appleton & Co., 1927.

Theodore Dreiser. "When Sails Are Furled," from *The Color of a Great City*. New York: Boni & Liveright, 1923, pp. 224-259.

Charles W. Leng and William T. Davis. *Staten Island and Its People A History* 1609-1929. New York: Lewis, 1930.

William Morris Barnes. *When Ships Were Ships and Not Tin Pots*. New York: Albert and Charles Boni, 1930.

Geoffrey T. Hellman. "A Reporter at Large, Sailors' Snug Harbor." *New Yorker*, May 26, 1934, pp. 67-68, 70-73.

O. W. Hicks. *Sea Tales From Sailors' Snug Harbor by O. W. Hicks An Inmate and a Member of N.E.D.A. 35 Years*. Privately printed. 1935.

James C. Healey. *Foc's'le & Glory Hole A Study of the Merchant Seaman and His Occupation*. New York: Oxford University Press, 1936.

Letters From John Pintard to His Daughter Eliza Noel Pintard Davidson 1816-1833. 4 Vols., New York: New-York Historical Society, 1940.

"Snug Harbor." *Saturday Evening Post*, June 15, 1940, pp. 16-18, 81, 82.

G. H. Coppers. "Snug Harbor." *Saturday Evening Post*, Vol. 226, February 27, 1954, p. 4.

Don C. Seitz. *The Sailors' Snug Harbor A History of Captain Robert Richard Randall's Foundation for the Toilers of the Sea*, 1959. MS. Board of Trustees Sailors' Snug Harbor.

Memorandum of the Trustees of Sailors' Snug Harbor in Opposition to Designation of Its Buildings as Landmarks Pursuant to Local Law No. 46 for the Year 1965. MS. Staten Island Historical Society.

J. J. Boies. "Melville's Staten Island Paradise." *Staten Island Historian*, Vol. 27, July-September 1966, pp. 24-28.

Harold D. Langley. *Social Reform In the U. S. Navy 1798-1862*. Chicago: University of Illinois Press, 1967.

"Squalls at Snug Harbor," *St. Louis Post Dispatch*, November 28, 1971, pp. 54-59.

Penelope McMillan. "Cast Off From Snug Harbor." *New York Sunday News*, January 28, 1973, pp. 18-21, 40.

Harmon H. Goldstone and Martha Dalrymple. *History Preserved, A Guide to New York City Landmarks and Historic Districts*. New York: Simon and Schuster, 1974.